"Why Do We Gotta Do This Stuff, Mr. Nehring?"

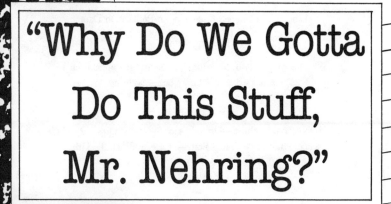

"Why Do We Gotta Do This Stuff, Mr. Nehring?"

Notes from a Teacher's Day in School

• • •

JAMES NEHRING

M. EVANS AND
COMPANY
NEW YORK

Library of Congress Cataloging-in-Publication Data

Nehring, James.

Why do we gotta do this stuff, Mr. Nehring? : notes from a
teacher's day in school / James Nehring.
p. cm.
ISBN 0-87131-574-2
1. High school teaching—United States—Case studies. 2. High
school students—United States—Case studies. I. Title.
LB1737.U6N44 1989   89-1352
373.11'02—dc19

M. Evans and Company, Inc.
216 East 49 Street
New York, New York 10017

BOOK DESIGN BY BARBARA M. BACHMAN

Manufactured in the United States of America
9 8 7 6 5 4 3 2 1

Contents

● ● ●

v

Foreword

Whether you are a parent, a veteran teacher, somebody who is studying to become a teacher, or somebody else, chances are you picked up this book because you have an interest in public education. Perhaps you have read reports on the condition of our schools by public-policy analysts and education "experts." Perhaps you are well versed in the reform-minded proposals outlined in those reports. Perhaps you are, yourself, involved in school reform in your community. But the fact that you picked up this book may indicate that all those big reports, despite their bigness, left some unanswered questions. And because you have an interest in public education, you've opened this book thinking maybe it will answer some of those questions.

This is a book by a teacher about school, about one day at school. It tells you what goes on at school between a teacher and the people he encounters there. It does not analyze national trends, it does not propose a nationwide program for school reform, it does not offer a history of American education. It cannot because it is not a big report supported by a private foundation, researched by a team of graduate students, and authored by an expert panel of policy analysts. It does not even include any footnotes. But it does give you a close-up view of teaching and learning in one school as seen by one teacher. And although it does not offer a program for school reform, it gestures toward certain truths about teaching and learning. In short, it does what the big books cannot do.

The setting for this book is Amesley Junior-Senior High School, a mainstream suburban school almost anywhere in the United States and a composite of the four public schools in which I have taught. Characters and events are thus thoroughly fictionalized, but in a very real way everything presented here has happened at one time or another.

Many people have contributed to the enterprise that finally culminated in this book, either by reading and commenting on the manuscript, giving encouragement, or promoting the finished work. In particular, I wish to thank Ruth McDowell, Jocelyn Jerry, John Piechnik, Dominick DeCecco, Donna Sutherland, Donald Sutherland, Joan Sutherland, Beth Nehring, Peter Nehring, Robert Nehring, Jr., Mary Jane Nehring, Robert Vogelbach, Jean Vogelbach, Barbara Nason, Theodore Sizer, William Finnegan, J. Briggs McAndrews, Dorothy Spelman, Virginia Foster, Richard Ahlstrom, Thomas McPheeters, Peggy O'Rourke, Michael Gallagher, the Wesleyan Writers Conference, and Ferris Mack (my editor at M. Evans and Company, Inc.). Also, I wish to acknowledge the work of Grant Wiggins, whose efforts with the Coalition of Essential Schools inspired the discussion of curriculum that appears in Chapter Eight.

Finally, there are certain individuals whose importance transcends thanks, and it is to them that I dedicate this book: to Laurie, my wife; to Mary and Robert Nehring, my mother and father; to my colleagues in the teaching profession, whose work is underpaid and underrecognized; and to my students, who are doing their best to grow up in this crazy world.

—James Nehring
Albany, NY
October 1988

"Why Do We Gotta Do This Stuff, Mr. Nehring?"

1.

A Minor Threat

• • •

Bernice Fleischman marches up the hall, announced by the steady, menacing click of her high heels on the masonry floor.

" 'Morning, Bernice." I look up from my desk, which is stationed where several hallways spill into a large, empty foyer—an intersection between classrooms, main office, library, cafeteria, guidance office. I serve here as traffic cop during first period, my "hall duty" for the day. At one end of this foyer is a row of heavy glass doors. The glass is laced with wire mesh. Beyond them are the concrete slabs of the smoking area, and beyond that, a big black parking lot which daily is worn by the large tires of yellow school buses. Hundreds of kids every morning at 7:15 flood the lot, then burst the glass doors and race down every hallway radiating from this foyer. Locker doors slam, big kids shove little kids, books fall to the floor, friends pick up conversations where they left off the day before, math homework is hastily done, doughnuts and Snickers bars make late breakfast.

But now it is 7:55, and the halls are quiet. First period is under way. Small groups of students on unassigned time breathe bright morning sun and cool April air out on the concrete, which is the designated student smoking area.

Indoors, several ne'er-do-wells grace the foyer with leather jackets and Sony Walkmans.

Bernice Fleischman says, "Good morning," and comes to parade rest. Left face. Tall, military in manner, and forever disapproving, she looks through the wire-mesh glass at Tony Mason, who is a student of hers in French One. Tony is performing on the air guitar. The act is apparently for his own enjoyment. As he stands outside a circle of boys playing Hacky Sack, none of the players looks at him or gestures in any way for him to join, yet Tony's lips explode silent musical notes each time he plucks the imaginary strings, which he does now frantically at the climax of a raucous solo. Tony's imaginary fans scream for more. His right hand reaches for the wa-wa, and his mouth circles around the distorted notes. The crowd is wild. Tony's knees bend, his back arches, and his head strains back in musical ecstasy. Suddenly his arms fall limp at his sides. The imaginary guitar hangs like a medallion from his neck, his entire person speaks creative exhaustion as the crowd applauds, standing on their seats.

"What a pit." Bernice shakes her head, pivots, and heads off down the hall. Click. Click. Click. Click.

Tony straightens up, puts his hands in his pockets, and looks around. Five boys stand in a loose circle on the white concrete. A blue-and-yellow leather sack, called a Hacky Sack, the size of a tennis ball and half filled with sand, rises a couple feet over the tallest boy's head, then falls spinning into the circle. A skinny blond boy wearing a Led Zeppelin T-shirt, Levi's jeans, and oversize high-top sneakers, laces untied, snaps the ball into the air again with a quick, subtle jerk of his left foot, popping the ball off his toe. His body remains loose and hunched. A cigarette sends up an undisturbed line of smoke from between the thumb and forefinger of his cupped left hand.

Next to the boys stands a resolute redbrick wall against which two girls sit basking in bright sunlight, radiating what warmth there is between wall and sidewalk. One smokes with nervous flicks from a long, red thumbnail. Conversation is animated, peppered with disapproving and pleading expressions.

Nearer the doors stands a green metal trash can. A husky boy who looks about seventeen with not quite shoulder-length straight black hair flicks ash into the open barrel. Since he lacks a companion, the trash can becomes one. He peers in the wide cavity, gives the can a kick, shuffles a little, looks down, takes a drag, looks up askance, and blows a controlled stream of smoke through the side of his mouth as if politely avoiding the face of a person who is not there.

Tony walks over to the trash can.

"Got a butt, man?" Soon Tony is inhaling comfortably from a Marlboro, air guitar on his back, a great rock and roll star having a backstage smoke with the lighting crew.

Indoors, high-pitched sounds spill from Amos Morley's Walkman into the open air of the foyer. Amos leans against a wall inside the foyer, reading a magazine, singing a cappella with notes that rise and fall not quite enough to carry the tune.

"Amos, can you hear me? Yo, Amos." I'm on patrol. Too much noise in the hall.

"Don't leave me, no. Don't leave me, no. Oh, it can't be. It can't be. Oh oh oh oh oh oh. Oh oh. Yeah yeah. Yeah oh no. Don't leave . . ."

I rise from my desk and walk over. "Amos, can you hear me? Earth to Amos. Come in, Amos."

Amos stirs like a guard caught sleeping. "Oh, yeah, man, what?" He fumbles the earphones from his head.

"Amos, do you think you could turn down your Walkman a few notches? I'm sure it can be heard halfway down the hall. We kind of like to keep things quiet during class."

"Oh, yeah, man, no problem. Like, I'm really sorry."

"Thanks." I walk away.

"And when we make love it's oh so good. It's oh so good. Oh oh oh oh oh oh. Oh oh. Yeah yeah. Yeah oh yeah."

The Walkman appeared in the U.S. around 1980. Its appearance in high schools was simultaneous, and it has since come to occupy, to preoccupy, the time and energy of school officials and teachers beyond any prediction, if predictions were made. It has become an epochal focus of malcontent between educators and the young.

Faculty meeting, Amesley High School, circa 1985. Principal Peters speaks.

"Next item: Walkmans. Or is it Walkmen? They're becoming a problem around the halls, on the bus, and, believe it or not, in class." Bill Fleming knits his brow. Skip Klein nods emphatically. Janet Degen rolls her eyes. Bernice Fleischman's shoulders straighten.

"We need to do something about them, but the question is what. Let me have some input on this. Yes, Al."

"Mr. Peters. Letting the kids walk around with their goddamn Walkmans is just one more abdication of our responsibility to maintain an orderly learning environment. I don't think that having kids bopping through the halls oblivious to the world with their Walkmans on is very conducive to learning, let alone wearing the things in class. My god, how can a kid possibly be tuned in to what I or his classmates are saying when Led Zeppelin is blasting away in his ears?"

"I agree." Skip Klein speaks. "I don't see why we should

4

have to allow them at all. Chester High School doesn't allow them, and they seem to get along fine without."

"Yeah." Roberta James speaks. "The problem is that here the kids know exactly who's boss. It's them, because we—the faculty and the administration—are simply not being firm and saying here's the line and you cannot cross over it. The kids will continue to do only what we allow them to. If we say no Walkmans and we enforce no Walkmans, there will be no Walkmans."

"Absolutely. They should be confiscated on sight," Bernice adds.

Peters: "It's sounding like the consensus is 'no Walkmans.' "

Al Short again: "Definitely. Let me tell a story. May I tell a story?

"Now, my students who wear these things—and I say 'wear,' because they're treated like some expensive article of clothing or trendy piece of jewelry for display . . . anyway, the ones who wear them tell me that they can hear perfectly well whatever is going on around them despite the fact that they've got these excess decibels just roaring in their eardrums, you know. Anyway, I'm standing in the lunch line the other day. I think it was Tuesday, and Amy Washington is standing in front of me. And she's bopping away to god knows what awful sexual thumping going on between her and her Walkman, and one of Mrs. Jane's cafeteria assistants walks up to us carrying one of those big stainless-steel urns of hot soup. And, you know, she's straining with this heavy thing, and she's got these oven mitts because the stuff is steaming hot, and she's being very mindful of the people around her, and she's saying, 'Hot soup, hot soup, please step aside.' Anyway, she gets to Amy Washington, who's into some kind of pelvic thrust at this point. Well, Amy is utterly oblivious to this potentially hazardous situation. And this lady is trying to be polite, and she says a little louder, 'I have hot soup here.' Amy clearly has no idea what's going on around her, and she swings her elbow into this woman's arm and the soup doesn't spill but splashes the poor woman's hand. Well, she manages to get through the line finally, but now she's got a burned hand. Meanwhile Washington has no idea what she's done. And the kids still have the gall to say, 'Oh, yeah, we can hear what's going on around us.' Bullshit."

"Truer words were never spoken." Chemistry teacher Tony Desista speaks. "And if I could just add quickly, these kids really add insult to injury because when you try to address them, you have to compete for their attention with the lead guitar, and then when they don't hear you, or don't listen in any case, they go out and do exactly what you warned them against, saying all the while that they heard every word you spoke to them. You know, I don't want to be held accountable if, God forbid, someday a kid burns himself with acid in lab because he didn't hear the directions over his tunes. I say ban them entirely."

"Hear, hear." Nods of assent. Scattered applause.

"Well, I don't know," Janet Degen says cautiously. Bernice straightens again. "I hear everything that everyone is saying. I know the kind of hazardous situations that Al and Tony are talking about, and I get as annoyed as anyone when I've got to compete with the Grateful Dead—which I can't even hear—for the attention of my students, but . . . I'm afraid of a knee-jerk reaction."

"Oh, come on, Janet!" Bill Pierce. "The only way to stop the problem is to eliminate the source."

"Okay, Bill. Fine. Let's say we ban Walkmans . . . just like we banned smoking. You remember what happened then? Because the kids couldn't smoke with our permission, they smoked without our permission. The bathrooms were a mess . . . one of them caught fire, remember? And George was booting kids out on suspension like there was no tomorrow. Banning Walkmans will not get rid of Walkmans, it will only make those kids who have them outlaws. And then we have to deal with another problem altogether."

Al: "Isn't that a little dramatic, Janet?"

Bill: "So what do you want, Janet? Do we keep the status quo and let the kids walk all over us and sabotage their education in the process?"

"Well, I don't know, but if we try to focus our kids' attention on learning by taking away the thing that's distracting them, then we may create a bigger distraction."

Andy Mullhauser careens into view from the far turn in the hall near the office of George Handelman, Assistant Principal. He steers his large, bony frame toward the foyer, slaps his oversize, unlaced work boots a little louder as he approaches. Eddie Whalen and Chug Van Duzer, who stand near the glass doors, look up.

"These fuckers think they can do whatever the fuck they goddamn please. Well, I don't want their shit, and I'm not gonna take their goddamn fucking shit, so fuck them!"

"Whoo, all right!" Eddie and Chug applaud and smile. Amos Morley looks up. Click. Turns off the Walkman. Their spontaneous show of support breaks the tension in Andy's face. He can't help laughing.

"Hey, so what the fuck? What are ya fuckin' gonna do, right?"

"Whadja get?" Chug asks.

"Five days' detention."

"Whoa, five days! Ole Handy's in a bad mood, I guess."

Their voices lower to inaudible chatter. Amos goes back

to his tunes. *Fuck* is commonplace in the halls. As long as
it is spoken softly and not addressed to a teacher, it is
ignored. If it is loud enough that a teacher hears it, and if
it is obvious to all in the vicinity that the teacher heard it,
then the teacher may do something. "Watch your language
in the hallways, please" or "Wait just a minute. Did I hear
what I think I heard?"

"Oh, no, Mr. Jones. I wouldn't use that kind of language."

"Good. See that you don't."

Encounters are often benign. Ritual. Formality. Homage
to standards that many students do not value, and which
teachers are reluctant to enforce. The message from popular
culture is clear. *Fuck* is okay. No big deal. It is a mild,
somewhat colorful oath at the same level of acceptability as
damn or *hell*. All students hear the message, some take it to
heart, and the rest do not protest loudly. Their adult role
models around school do not protest loudly, either. The
adult role models say they cannot enforce standards that
society does not enforce.

"Fuck you."

"Excuse me? What did you say?"

"Oh, nothing. I didn't mean anything by it."

"No. I heard what you said." One day Ray Alvaredo,
math teacher, decides to make a stand against the casual
use of what some still consider strong, offensive language.

"I'm sorry. I really didn't mean it. It wasn't about
you."

"What is your name, son?"

"Ohhhh, maaaaaan . . ."

"Your name."

"Peter Thurston."

"Peter, you can explain yourself to Mr. Handelman in
the morning."

* * *

"Peter, here at Amesley High School we like to think that there's a certain level of decorum that everyone, students and adults, adheres to."

"Yes, Mr. Handelman."

"Peter, why did you do it?"

"I don't know, Mr. Handelman. You're right, and I don't usually use that kind of language.

"Peter, you're obviously a good student. This is the first time I've ever seen you in here. Let's make it the last. Now beat it."

"Thanks, Mr. Handelman."

Maybe Ray was in a bad mood. Maybe he felt an upsurge of impotence. Maybe he took Peter's remark as just one more act of rebellion against adult order and decency. Maybe he momentarily forgot that fewer and fewer people care that students say *fuck* casually in the hallway—or that teachers have been heard using the same word when the copy machine jams. Maybe Ray was just plain fed up with the general state of chaos in public education and saw an opportunity to do his part, however small, in restoring order.

Greater minds, I am sure, have attempted to explain the cultural implications of the increasing use of *fuck* in the hallways, and the increasing volume at which it is increasingly spoken. Fact is, the word is part of most young people's language environment these days. It is surprising that more students do not speak it with the ease that movie characters and some of their peers do. Yes, to say *fuck* in the hallways is an act of rebellion. But rebellion is nothing new. To say "Fuck you" to a person is abusive and mean.

But abuse and meanness are not new, either. To say "Fuck this" to the photocopy machine *is* new, but only because the photocopy machine is new. Youthful rebellion, abusiveness, meanness, and anger are not new. Neither is *fuck*, for that matter.

Meanwhile Andy Mullhauser seems to have cooled off. I walk half the distance between us.

"Andy, could I talk to you for a minute?" He walks over.

"Whatever it is, I did not do it."

"Andy, the language you use in private is your business. I don't care about that. But this is a public hallway here, and some people, believe it or not, are still offended by strong language. So I would ask please that you not use that kind of language in the halls, okay?"

"Oh. Okay. Is that it?"

"That's it."

On the desk at my hallway station is a stack of "things to do": a memo from the social studies department chair; a magazine en route through the department; an overdue notice from the library; what seems like the third printout of second-quarter grades; a camp-counselor recommendation that Peter Weinstein asked me to complete; a half-written work sheet on urbanization in South Asia. Underneath "things to do" is "papers to correct," seventy-two of them (if everybody did it) from my three social studies classes. Amazingly, there are no papers from my two English classes.

Underneath "papers to correct" is "misc.," a folder with essays turned in late, makeup quizzes and tests, and other student work that has drifted to the deepest recess of paper correctiondom.

Where to begin . . .

A mature-looking boy, whose name I do not know, floats out of the cafeteria, balancing in each hand a cup of coffee with a Danish on top.

"Excuse me, sir." (I discovered long ago that *sir* and *ma'am* are quickest to get a student's attention. Sometimes *yo* is good.) "Would you mind finishing those up in the cafeteria?"

"They aren't for me."

"Well, would you mind telling whoever they're for that they should come to the cafeteria for their breakfast?"

"*Mr. Bigg* asked me to bring these up to the writing lab."

"Oh . . . okay." The coffee cups float past, one dripping. Al Corrigan, day custodian, rounds the bend on cue.

"See, that's the reason we don't like kids eating in the hallways," says Al.

"Yeah. Dave Bigg *asked* that kid to bring coffee and Danish up to the writing lab."

"Oh." Al's hollow "oh" really says Dave Bigg ought to follow the same rules everyone else does.

Amy VanderSee steps into the hall, doughnut in hand, sees us, hesitates, proceeds.

"Ah, Amy, would you mind finishing that up in the cafeteria?"

"How come *he* gets to go by and I can't?" Bigg's errand boy is just rounding the turn at the end of the hall.

"Well . . . Mr. Bigg asked him to get coffee."

"Oh, so teachers get to do it but we can't?"

"It would appear that way."

Amy stuffs the rest of the doughnut in her mouth. "That sucks."

"That's a mouthful." She doesn't like my joke.

Al shakes his head and leaves.

"Things to do." I look up, hopeful of another distraction. All's quiet in the smoking area. No noise in the halls. I look down.

11

Mr. Nehring,
 Please schedule an appointment at your earliest convenience
for a post-observation conference.
> Sincerely,
> Donald Rickover,
> Chairman, Social Studies Department

This conference will be a pleasant affair, I think. The
old admiral will tell me how impressed he was with my
class. He will say that my use of structured work sheets
showed excellent preparation, the students responded well
to my questions (excellent questioning strategy), the material was appropriate to the syllabus and challenged students at their level of ability, and the bulletin-board displays
were highly educational. Then he will make a few de rigueur
recommendations for improvement: I could have gone into
greater depth on . . . I might consider using the overhead
projector for . . . Then I will say how thoughtful and com-
plimentary his report is, we will make jovial small talk, and
that will be that. Nice pat on the back. You don't get many
in teaching, so you relish the ones you get. I make a mental
note to schedule the meeting. Then the admiral's commu-
niqué goes to the bottom of the stack.

A student appears from the semidarkness of the hallway
running at full speed. He is by me. I call after him. "Yo,
guy, slow down!" He disappears at full speed around the
far turn.

I look down at my stack of papers. I look up.

Boy reappears on return leg of journey. Still at full speed.
This time I am ready. I rise and form a human roadblock.
He slows momentarily—ready to submit, I wrongly inter-
pret. Having scanned out the weak point of my roadblock,
he is by me. "I have more important things to do than walk."
Protest or apology? Anyway, he is gone.

"Things to do." I check my name off the routing list for *Social Education*, the official journal of the National Council for the Social Studies. Slick, well-researched, scholarly articles, I think. How many of the people who write these articles are schoolteachers? Professor of Education and Anthropology at the University of Texas, Chair of Teacher Education and Curriculum at Stanford, Associate Professor of Education at Penn State, Professor of History at the University of Colorado, Supervisor of Social Studies Education for the Wisconsin Department of Public Instruction, Professor, Professor Emeritus, On Leave from Arizona State, Professor, Professor . . . Well, guys, nice articles. Yes, the Committee for Tenure Review approves. . . . As for us folks here in the infantry, it's all a little high-sounding. I slide *Social Education* to the bottom of the stack.

Tall, lanky boy (I think) steps through the doorway from the smoking area, walks to adjacent wall, leans against it, slides to floor, head hung. MINOR THREAT, his T-shirt declares. His hair is cut short, almost crew-cut, except for a three-inch-wide strip just over his forehead. It is almost a foot long and hangs like a narrow veil down the middle of his face to about his chin. A cartoon comes to mind: Elephant trying to hide from hunters on safari yanks up a seedling and holds it in front of his face, his body spilling out in all directions from behind this very inadequate camouflage. *I can't see you*, the elephant thinks, *therefore you can't see me*.

Minor Threat does not move. He looks hung over. Things to do . . .

Mr. Nehring_____ ,
   Your library material
      The African Experience

was due on _____3/25_____

Please return it.

Robert Berkowicz, our librarian, is forthright. No bureaucratic jargon here. It's overdue. Return it. This little slip was the cause of some humor at my expense in homeroom this morning.

7:40 A.M., Homeroom 25.

"Okay, everybody. Fan-mail time. From guidance for Joe Tanner." I pass the note back. "From guidance for Amy Karpov. Ah, from the library. Overdue books. *For Whom the Bell Tolls.*"

"Bingo." A voice from the rear of the room. "That's me, Mr. Nehring. But you can throw it out. I already returned it."

"No, Jill, *you* can throw it out. Here."

"*The American Political Experience.* Ooh. One, two, three weeks overdue. No takers? Mr. Bill Addison, here. If you do not return this book, they will take away your driver's license."

"Oh, my god, a fate worse than death!"

"*The African Experience.* No takers? Five, six, seven days overdue."

"It's on your desk, Mr. Nehring."

"They're gonna take away your driver's license."

As I serve my duty in the hall, *The African Experience* is still on my desk. I will return it during my unassigned time later today.

I am told that the effective manager will go through his "in" pile exactly once, dispensing with matters immediately in the order that they appear. That would be fine if I were allowed to get up out of my seat to retrieve *The African*

Experience and bring it immediately to the library. I guess the wisdom on effective management does not take "hall duty" into account.

The overdue notice goes to the bottom of things to do, and my pink grade sheets fall to the floor and scatter. Oversize and cumbersome, waiting to be "reconciled" with the grades in my plan book, they represent a computer advance and the sort of tedious clerical task that offers an opportunity for math error with each of its several hundred little illegible dot-matrix numbers. I pick them up off the floor, fold once, and lay them carefully at the bottom of "things to do."

I come inexorably to my student essays, based on the following current-event item: terrorist bomb explodes in downtown bank in European city during banking hours. Three killed. Many injured. Terrorists phone newspaper, say bomb was set to go off after banking hours. They apologize to families of dead but warn that persons who participate in capitalist system must assume responsibility for their actions. Police chief swears before grief-stricken widow to bring bombers to justice. Assignment: Write two letters to the editor, one from the widow, one from a terrorist.

Esther Cole writes:

Dear Mr. Editer,
   I am writting to say that I am the widow of of the man who was killed. He should be braught to justice. He is a crimanal.
                                        Sincerly,
                                        Esther Cole

Dear Mr. Editer,
   I am writing to say I am the terrist who bommed your bank. You deserve it. Your capalist sistym is no good. You have to much money

Sincerly,
Esther Cole

Andrew Harmon writes:

To the Editor:
Yesterday, I became the victim of a terrorist attack. My husband was in the National Bank at 11:00 A.M. He was killed in the explosion while I waited outside. I suddenly became one of those people that you see grief-stricken in a photograph on the front page of the paper, one of those people that you hope you will never become. My life is now changed forever. My one obsession has suddenly become and will remain the pursuit of the terrible cowards who killed my husband. How many more victims will there be?

Andrew Harmon

To the Editor:
The Red Guardians take full responsibility for yesterday's offensive against one of this community's citadels of capitalism. All acts in the struggle to liberate the people from the yoke of oppression are self-justified. All members of this society who participate in the capitalist system share responsibility for the oppression it has created. We regret the loss of life, but our struggle has always been of necessity a violent one.

Long Live the Revolution!
The Red Guardians

Andrew and Esther are in the same class. Our current school district superintendent does not believe in "tracking." All kids should be taught in the same class, he says. Tracking stigmatizes students, according to the research. It arbitrarily lowers teacher expectations. "Heterogeneous grouping," he says, is where it's at. Therefore, as his first major policy act as new superintendent two years ago, he

16

decreed that all students, except for about the lowest ten percent in each class, would be heterogeneously grouped. Thus Esther and Andrew wind up together in my second-period social studies class.

Classes at Amesley High School used to be "homogeneous"; that means kids were placed in different classes depending on how able and motivated we figured they were. This is also called tracking. Some schools have five tracks. We had three. I have even heard of one high school that at the peak of enrollment in the early seventies had fourteen tracks. Imagine trying to argue that Johnny belongs in track nine, not ten or eight.

Anyway, at Amesley High, homogeneous grouping is no more. At least until the superintendent, current or future, becomes persuaded by the other body of research that sees merit in tracking. Meanwhile the teachers are up in arms since they've been teaching to tracked groups for the last million years and all of a sudden are expected to teach both Andrew and Esther in the same class at the same time. There's been a good deal of scrambling at Amesley as teachers try out any and all varieties of lesson plans that will simultaneously challenge Andrew to, say, understand Marx's theory of class struggle while enlightening Esther with the correct spelling for *wuz*.

But it has not been all bad news. Desperation has bred creativity. Alice Berry and Tom Albright created and produced an original faculty room skit, "Heterosexual Groping." There was the anonymous misdelivery to our superintendent's office of a tankload of homogenized milk. Some teachers have even devised novel teaching strategies to reach as much of their heterogeneous nontracked class as possible. My own solution has been to have the most capable kids do individual projects while kids who sort of understand tutor those classmates who clearly have no idea what is going on. This effort even resulted in a scholarly-sounding paper entitled "Peer Tutoring in the Heterogeneously Grouped Class." This thoughtfully researched article, complete with impressive-looking bibliography, was rejected by the editor of *Social Education*, who obviously does not know good work when he sees it.

Minor Threat gets up, looks around, and sashays out of the foyer, down the hall.

He has just entered the library! Possibly to read *Catcher in the Rye*. Probably to read *High Times*.

I should know better. He is probably a thoughtful, sensitive kid who turns in his assignments on time and earns good grades. He maintains a facade of youthful decadence and rebellion only to provoke and frustrate adult prejudices simultaneously. Like mine. Maybe he'll read *Sports Illustrated*.

No. I've got it. He has been assigned *Catcher in the Rye* by his radical-minded English teacher. He will read the Cliff Notes.

Back to Esther and Andrew.

Esther can't write and she can't read. Well, she can put apparently semi-intelligible sentences onto paper, and she can pronounce aloud the words she sees in her textbook, if she bothers to look at them.

This is leading me to a discussion of declining test scores, which I was hoping I could avoid, since no doubt there already have been many fine, well-researched articles in *Social Education* on just this subject. I can't imagine I'll add anything original, but there may be merit in adding still another voice to the chorus.

I am told that SAT scores have been drifting downward

for about twenty years. Therefore we conclude that student math and verbal ability in general is declining. Right? Not so fast. The SAT has always been taken by only a small minority of high-school students—college-bound kids. Also, that small minority swelled slightly during the 1970s at a time when there was generally more money for kids to go to college. Also, SAT scores have increased ever so slightly during the last several years. Also, the test has been criticized as culturally biased. What do we make of this? What I make of it is that test scores declined through the seventies in part because more disadvantaged minority kids were taking the SAT. Then, when money for college began to tighten up during the Reagan years, those disadvantaged kids stopped taking the test, and scores began to rise. Some concluded, I think wrongly, that our kids were getting smarter again, that all our educational reforms were starting to pay off. What do I conclude? I conclude that the SAT gives us questionable information about a small minority of students.

Similar problems exist with other so-called standardized tests. There may be a principle here. To the extent that a test is standardized and validated, test results are questionable. And the more loudly its proponents argue its validity, the harsher its critics will slam the test. I have seen this happen again and again, in face-offs between parent and teacher, superintendent and school board, principal and union, professor and schoolteacher, state education offical and local administrator, and so on.

Is the converse true? I mean, is there a test that claims no standard, about which there could be no criticism? Recently I was drinking coffee in the faculty room with some of my cohorts when in flew Joe Burtis. Joe was mad. He said, "I can't believe these stupid assholes. I've been giving the same goddamn differential equations test for ten years, and every year the little bastards do worse. What am I supposed to do?"

Another occasion. I am talking with the Admiral about a test on ancient Africa that we both have just administered to our ninth-grade classes. Rickover says, "You know, I made up this test years ago for our average-ability groups, and now it's challenging to our top performers."

Yet another. An end-of-the-year cocktail party. No, scratch that. Teachers don't have cocktail parties. An end-of-the-year free happy hour sponsored by the union. I am talking with Drew Muldoon, biology teacher. "So, Drew, how did your kids do on the Regents Exam?"

"Same as usual. Worse than last year."

Burtis, Rickover, and Muldoon have each been teaching for at least a quarter century at Amesley High. They are not, generally speaking, cynics, and abusive language notwithstanding, they care about kids and their education. They have all taught at Amesley High for their entire careers in education. Amesley, during that whole time, has been a racially homogeneous, socioeconomically advantaged community—a rich white suburb. But this sounds like I'm trying to validate my testing method, thus inviting criticism. So I'll stop.

I'm bored. 8:27. Ten minutes to go. Not enough time to correct papers. I rise and cross the hall to a display of watercolors hanging on the wall, which I stupidly have not noticed until just now.

The pieces are by David Silverstein, a senior. There are eight, suspended by fishing line at different heights along a span of wall several paces wide. David has been studying some modern art history. One piece looks a lot like Dali's *Persistence of Memory*, and several others show drooping or liquid portrayals of hard, real objects on surreal landscapes.

The rest are cubist, with an active vibrating quality. *Guernica, Three Musicians.*

Well, they're copies. David is mimicking what he sees in art books. No big deal. They are good copies, though, carefully done. He demonstrates not only knowledge of surrealism and cubism, he shows some competence with composition, color, shadow, dimension. The best writers start by copying the work of writers they admire. David is copying the work of artists he admires. An appropriate activity for an artist at David's stage. Not so bad, I guess.

Three girls come dallying down the hallway. They see me and cast a glance at David's work.

"Weird."

"Pretty bizarre."

"Pretty modernistic."

No, pretty old-fashioned, I feel like saying. Did you know this kind of stuff was being done when your grandfather was a kid? Pete Gambone, English teacher, sallies by, coffee in hand. Stops. Looks. Silence. Yes, Pete. So?

"It's no wonder our students are so troubled." He leaves.

Pete, I want to say, that that is a real idiotic statement. You take your poetry classes to museums. You appreciate the kind of art this student is copying. You know why he's copying it. You are a culturally literate person.

I contrive Pete's reply: He's copying it because he identifies with it. He identifies with it because, like the people who made this stuff, he is sick.

No (me talking), he is copying it because it is what he sees at the back of the archaic art-history books this school has. He thinks he is the avant garde. He thinks he is jarring artistic conventions. He thinks he is ahead of his time. And I guess at Amesley High School, he is.

Great artists are sometimes greatly disturbed, Nehring.

David Silverstein is not disturbed. He is a kid with some

talent, being a little rebellious, trying to shock, trying to upset, and apparently—amazingly—doing it.

My self-serving little reverie is interrupted. Bill Middleton, art teacher, comes down the hall. Perfect.

"Bill, got a minute?"

"Ahm . . ."

I take his arm. "What do you think of David Silverstein's work?"

"I don't think it's very good."

"Then why is it hanging in the hall?"

"Because Amy VanderSee didn't want hers put up and we needed something for this month."

"Well, everybody walks by, and they say things like 'Weird,' 'Sick,' 'This person is disturbed.' What do you make of comments like that?"

"What do I make of them? Well . . . this kind of stuff is nothing new. Some of it *is* shocking. It's outlandish in the best sense of the word. But those are intended effects of a controlled process. It doesn't mean the artist is sick."

"Thank you."

"May I go?"

"You may go."

So these kids are not sick, I think. They are trying to shock us. David shocks us with watercolors. Minor Threat with his veil of hair. The kids in the smoking area with cigarettes. The stereo boxes. The Walkmans. A controlled process. And when we adults get the volts and jump in fright, they say, "Yippee!" An intended effect. But none of this is new. It *was* going on when their grandfathers were kids. It was going on long before that. It was going on two thousand years ago when Socrates's students were knocking over vases in the Agora and yanking at each other's tunics. And when Socrates got bungled up and couldn't think of the next question, the kids would say, "Yippee!" (In Greek.)

I look at my watch. It is three minutes later than the last time I looked at my watch. Yesterday I reprimanded Billie Oates. The kids were doing individual work at their desks. Billie was doodling and looking out the window and looking at her watch. Use your time constructively, Billie.

All is quiet. I think about the day ahead: eight forty-five-minute "periods" with five minutes between each for recuperation. According to my schedule, I teach five academic classes, serve two supervisory duties, eat lunch, and get one "free" period, which makes nine periods in an eight-period day. (This could happen only in public education.) Actually, period nine rotates, which means that it slowly descends through the schedule, replacing a different class each day until on "A" day, it, too, rotates out. I have been teaching at Amesley for seven years, and I still find this confusing.

Thoughts turn to second period: Gandhi's nonviolent movement in India. In today's class, students will imagine that they are Indians in the 1930s and 1940s. They will be faced with situations that Indians faced and will have to decide how they could resist British domination. Then we will discuss the ways Gandhi resisted the British. What ethic guided Gandhi's program for social reform? (Andrew: "The Jainist concept of ahimsa, or reverence for life." Esther: "What's a ethic?") In what ways did mass participation in organized acts of civil disobedience help the cause of Indian independence? (Andrew: "Peaceful demonstrations by the Indians focused the attention of the world on the cause of Indian independence and gave the Indian people a moral upper hand to the British, who appeared in the eyes of the world to be more and more brutish." Esther: "Huh?") The lesson is planned; the props are in place in the room. I have taught this lesson for several years. Each year I get out a few more bugs, and it runs pretty well now.

This year I want to revise the discussion questions a little to include more simple questions so that Esther won't be completely star-struck. With ten minutes I have just enough time to make up a good list.

A crescendo of chair sliding, foot scraping, book shuffling, and talking at the end of the hall. A class full of seniors streams through Judy Bickel's doorway. I check my watch: 8:31. Six minutes to go. Why is Judy letting these kids out six minutes early? This disorder must be contained, I think like a cop. This commotion will disrupt every class on the hallway: students will look at watches, close books, begin conversations; dramatic climaxes of lectures will be missed; teachers will yell at kids for being rude; kids will think teachers are jerks for being too demanding; assignments will be missed. This disorder must be contained, I think, like a teacher. I rise and jog toward the mob.

"Hey, guys, how come you're out in the hall? It's only eight thirty-one."

"The sub let us out early."

"Oh." I should have known.

"Well, listen, you wanna keep the noise down a little, please?"

"Mumble mumble yea mumble no problem mumble mumble."

"And you wanna turn off the stereo box? You're not even supposed to have one of those in school."

Click. "Mumble mumble asshole mumble mumble."

"Whoa. Wait a minute. Did I hear what I think I heard?"

"Oh, no, Mr. Nehring. I wouldn't use that kind of language."

I think about Ray Alvaredo.

I think about Peter Thurston.

I think about rules, kids, rebellion, meanness and abuse, stereo boxes, Walkmans, George Handelman, heterogeneous grouping, *fuck*, Eddie Murphy, Andy Mullhauser, declining test scores, TV, Led Zeppelin, the copy machine, Eddie Whalen and Chug Van Duzer, Hacky Sack, Tony Mason, and the air guitar.

I think about Bernice Fleischman and Ronald Reagan. I think about the SAT. I think about Esther and Andrew and the superintendent of schools and the commissioner of education and disapproving custodians and Socrates, and I think about the smoking area and *Sports Illustrated*.

And I think about Minor Threat.

"No. Wait a minute. I *heard* what you said."

2.

Groups

• • •

8:42 A.M. Second period has just begun. I round the last turn to my hallway and my classroom. The corridor is clear of students, who at this moment are seated in columns and rows behind closed doors amid much throat clearing, shuffling of books, and sharpening of pencils in anticipation of lessons in math and English and biology and American history and Spanish and French and . . .

I notice a great clot of students—my second-period students—midway down the hall; ninth-graders pacing and spinning and hovering and buzzing like a swarm of bees dancing their cryptic bee-body language around the mouth of the hive. Ninth-graders speak a cryptic body language to which anyone older has no entrée. All memory of it is lost somewhere in the summer between ninth and tenth grades.

"He's coming," says a voice on the edge of the swarm, and the motion at mid-hall visibly picks up.

Dave Bigg, chief ward of the writing center and my next-door neighbor here on the ninth-grade hall, stands in his doorway and eyes me like I was a truant schoolboy treading remorsefully toward the school door. And thus I feel, but Billy Abrams, owner of the boom box and caster of aspersions, had to be shown that rules can be enforced and that abuse is not always tolerated, and I was the only one there to do it, and so I escorted him to George Handelman's office, and so we waited awkwardly, silently, outside George's door because George was with another student, and so in the fullness of time it was our turn, and so I explained to George what was what, and Billy interrupted me, and so there were raised voices and gnashing of teeth, and so I left Billy with George, and so I hastened to my classroom, full on the other side of the building, and so I did arrive late to my classroom, and so I was remiss in one duty in order to serve another, but now I am here, composed and ready, so now you may go about your own business, Dave. Dave disappears into his room. I turn to my students.

"Yes, I am here. No, I did not have a heart attack. No, there was no death in the family. No, I didn't walk through the glass doors. No, you don't get a sub. You get me." I insert the key, turn it, and push the door open.

"Where's your pass, Mr. Nehring?"

"Wise guy." I bop Aaron Hughes on the head playfully as students scatter toward their chairs.

Hurrying toward my desk, I hope to seize this moment of settling to glance over my lesson plan. What *am* I teaching these kids today? Usually I am able to rehearse my second-period lesson on my way back to the classroom from hall duty. Today, though, I have been preoccupied with Billy's bravado and my consequent lateness to class. I strain to recall the plan, even the topic, but I cannot. My mind is elsewhere. I must find my plan written on the back of an old quiz. I thought it was on my blotter. Not there. Top drawer? Not there. Filing cabinet? Which one? South Asia. Yes, that's it, I'm teaching about South Asia. That's my topic. I look in the filing cabinet. Not there. Students are pretty well settled in their seats. As I look around the room there is relative quiet. Some students even have pencil in hand, as if ready to take notes. Why can't they be this way every other day when I know where my lesson plan is? I start to go through my other desk drawers. Silence falls. They know something is wrong. I'll be better off admitting it.

"I'll be happy to teach you all today if I can find my notes." I move back to the filing cabinet.

"That's okay, Mr. Nehring. We don't mind just hangin' out."

"I'm sure."

"Can we talk?"

"As long as you talk about social studies." I slide another drawer open.

"Oh, yeah. That's all we ever talk about."

"It is? Well, my goodness, then why don't you tell me about the history of British colonialism in India?"

"Sure."

"Well . . . I'm waiting."

"Okay. The British, see, wanted these spices. And so they went to India."

"How did they know how to get there?" I ask.

"Well, I guess they looked at a map."

"True enough. Whose map did they look at?" I find the plan on top of the filing cabinet, lying among papers to be corrected.

"Vasco da Gama's!" cries a voice from the back row. It is David Genovese. Gallantly he has come to the rescue of Molly McNulty, who has been chirping precociously from the front row until the last question, which seems to have exhausted her knowledge of Indian history.

"Very good, David. Tell me more about old Vasco."

"Well, like, he's this guy . . . from Portugal, who sailed around Africa . . . in 1498 . . ."

"*Ooh aah*," goes the class.

". . . and he went on to India . . . and then he came back and told everybody all about it and made a map and made like photocopies for all his friends."

"Photocopies?"

"Yeah, that's what you told us yesterday."

"Oh . . . well, I was kidding. You couldn't make photocopies in 1498, because there was no place to plug in the photocopy machines because people didn't know yet how to use electricity. So they didn't have wall outlets. In fact, they didn't have photocopy machines, either. But I am truly impressed, class. Next time you tell me you talk about social studies in your spare time, I'll believe you. Now I have an important announcement. You have good luck today. I've found my notes. History may proceed."

The class groans in unison. They are good kids. And they are now ready to get down to work. I couldn't have *planned* a better opener than the one that emerged spontaneously from the loss of my notes and Molly McNulty's good-natured truculence. Serendipity has a place in teaching.

Today's lesson, which happily I now remember as I glance over my notes, is about Mohandas Gandhi's non-violent methods of political reform.

"I have a question for you today. How do you win a war without putting up a fight?" Blank stares. "I mean, is it possible to win a war when your enemy is firing at you without shooting back?"

"No way," says Andy Newcomb.

Randy Emon's hand goes up.

"Yes, Randy."

"I s'pose if you run away."

"Okay, let's suppose you run away. What may happen to you?"

"You get shot in the back," says Andy.

"That's one possibility," I say.

"Or you get away and don't get shot," says Tom Conners, who sits on Andy's left.

"Yeah," says Andy, "but even if you get away, you still didn't win. You might get caught later and be a prisoner of war or get shot or something."

"Which means you haven't won the war," I add, to round off Andy's thought.

"Right," says Andy.

"Well, then," I say, "that brings us back to our original question. Do you think it's possible to win a war without fighting back?"

Scattered nos around the room.

"Well, today we're going to begin to learn about somebody who tried to do just that, a person in India who decided he was going to try to get the British out of India without starting a war, even though the British were armed and had no intention of leaving."

"You mean we're gonna talk about Gandhi?" says Esther Cole from the middle of the room.

"Yes, ma'am. Mohandas K. Gandhi," I say dramatically.

"I saw the movie," says Esther. "It was dumb."

"How many of you saw the movie?" I ask. About a third of the class raises their hands.

"It was really long," says Ed.

"And boring," adds another critic.

"Hey, maybe we could go on a field trip." It's Molly McNulty, always quick with a good idea.

"Yeah. We could all go see *Gandhi*. It would be educational," says Ed.

"But I thought *Gandhi* was dumb and long and boring," I say.

"That's okay. It wasn't really so bad."

"Well, I tell you what. If you do a good job with the

work I've planned for you, we'll see about watching part
of *Gandhi* on video."

"Oh, cool," they answer.

"I have a handout for you that is going to help us get
started."

Leading an educational discussion with ninth-graders requires deft helmsmanship. The crew has a natural tendency
to steer left or right when the destination is straight ahead.
Mutiny may result if the helmsman pushes too hard on the
rudder to get back on course, but disaster will strike the
ship if the crew steers alone. What's needed is constant,
gentle vigilance. A little push this way. A little that way.
So far today our ship is more or less on course.

I pass out the paper.

I have decided in advance that I will allow students to
complete the handout in small groups. We will then reassemble as a class, they will offer their answers, and I will
explain civil disobedience, passive resistance, boycott, and
strike in the context of Gandhi's nonviolent movement.

Groups. I often have my students spend class time working in groups. I think it's good for them in a lot of ways.
One of my goals as a teacher is to get my students to take
seriously and talk seriously about important ideas—with
each other. Having them discuss civil disobedience and the
like in a controlled classroom setting, i.e. where I get to
say, "No you can't talk about that, but yes, you should talk
about this," is good practice. Also, talk has a way of mul-
tiplying creative ideas—two heads are better than one because of the happy possibilities of randomly combined
ideas—serendipity again. Groups are also a stimulus to action and engagement. Being faced with two or three peers
at a distance of two or three feet is just threatening enough,
and just exciting enough, to get most kids doing something.
I offer directions hopefully to see that what they do is the

something I want them to do. Finally, experience tells me that only in the rarest of circumstances (e.g., test, parent conference) can ninth-graders sustain calm, silence, and concentration for more than a few minutes before breaking into oral or physical activity.

So I do a lot of groups. And there is much talk. And most of the talk is what it's supposed to be about, but sometimes it's not, which means I need to rethink how I make the groups.

Figuring out how to group students for a small group activity is an interesting teacher problem. It involves so many of those things about which teachers learn in teacher-education courses and claim they never use but which they use all the time: adolescent psychology, group dynamics, communication theory, teaching methodology. Let's suppose I say to my students, "Okay, kids, work with anybody you want for the next ten minutes and get this done." I sometimes do just that. The ensuing events in my classroom will probably be very different than if I say, "Okay, kids, get with all the people in your row for the next ten minutes and get this done." And things will probably be different again if I decide in advance what the groups will be and arrange them so that each group has one very able student, one slow student, and one in between. Or suppose I put all the bright kids in one group, all the slow kids in another, and everybody else in another. Or all the kids who work hard together and all the goof-offs together. Or all the shy kids together and the outgoing kids together. Or, dare I say, boys against girls? How about the black kids against the white kids?

Sorry, I got carried away.

Each way of organizing the class produces its own set of effects. I made a big mistake my first year of teaching. In the first week of school I let my slow class make their own groups without considering what I was doing. Everybody was with his or her friends. All the rowdy boys were together, all the chatty girls, all the quiet and serious boys, all the quiet and serious girls. And several individuals who felt uncomfortable joining any of their classmates' unofficial fraternal societies remained at their desks, marking the column and row, now vanished, as students steered their desks together and apart, crashing against walls and other desks in bumper-car fashion. The groups, such as they were, eventually coalesced, except that like electrons changing orbitals, an occasional student suddenly would spin away from one group and join another. I gave my students their task. I went from group to group offering advice, making directions clear, explaining difficult vocabulary words. And despite my best, albeit novice, efforts to carry on with the lesson, the lesson became overwhelmed by the group dynamics.

"Yo, Cindy. Jeff says he likes you."

"Well, tell Jeff I don't like him."

"Well, then, how come I saw you sittin' together outside the mall on Friday?"

"Did not."

"Did too."

"Did not. You're stupid."

"Hey, Angie."

"What?"

"How come John's hangin' around with Ann Marie?"

"I don't know and I don't care."

"I bet ya don't."

"That's right, I don't."

Given the climate, even my quiet and serious types lost interest.

"You hear about the trout that Mulrooney pulled out of Lower Valley Creek?"

"Yeah, it ain't true. He's always sayin' stuff."

"I saw a picture—him and the trout."

"It's prob'ly a fake."

Thus were antagonisms deepened, rumors dispatched, and tall tales told, but little did the planned lesson impress the hearts and minds of my class that day. In fact, having fostered some volatile alliances, I spent much of the remaining school year undoing the effect of one day's innocent attempt at groups.

Anyway, in planning today's lesson on Gandhi, I consider my past mistakes and victories with groups. And wishing to create a climate more reasoned than impassioned, I decide to arrange today's groups according to the one method that is blind to friendship and enmity, gender and race. I have my students count off by fives. Thus are created five groups of five. And my students are off to work.

"Mr. Nehring?"

"Yes, Christine."

"I don't get it."

"Well, what don't you get?"

"The whole thing."

"Hmm . . . well, do you know what you're supposed to be doing with the other people in this group?"

"We're supposed to do this." She holds up the handout.

"Right. Have you read the directions?"

"Yeah."

"And what do the directions tell you to do?"

"That's what I don't get."

"I see. Well, let me see if I can put it in different words. This handout describes four situations that the Indian people faced all the time back in the days when the British were running their country."

"Uh-huh."

"Now, I want you to imagine that you are an Indian

living back in those days and you don't like the fact that the British are always telling you what to do in your own country."

"Uh-huh."

"So you want to get rid of the British. Problem is, you don't like violence and bloodshed. So you have to try to figure out some way of getting back at the British in each of these situations without resorting to violence and bloodshed."

"So, like, I can't shoot anybody?"

"Like, you can't shoot anybody, right."

"Oh, I get it."

"Good. Why don't you try the first one on your own, and then I'll come back and see how you're doing."

"Okay."

Especially with slower kids, their frustration at not being able to figure out what's going on is made worse by their inability to explain where they got lost.

"What don't you get?"

"I don't get the whole thing."

So Teacher has two jobs. First, Teacher must find out where student got lost—which sometimes takes a long time—then Teacher must set student straight. Teacher must nurture special skill, which I will call backward thinking. Here is a situation that requires backward thinking.

Michael Summer raises his hand on the far side of the room. I leave Christine to help Michael.

"Yes, Michael. What can I do for you?"

"I'm lost."

At this point I decide not to ask where he got lost, because chances are he will say, "I don't know. If I knew, then I wouldn't be lost," and because that little exchange will irritate both sides, it is better left out. I'm not quite sure, however, how to set Michael back on course, but I need to say something and not just stand there looking stupid because, after all, I'm the teacher.

So I say, "Well, Michael. Worry not. We will find you and set you back on course."

What I must do is locate a probable point at which Michael became lost, describe this point to him, and find out whether he recognizes it. So what are some probable points? Thinking backward, they are one of the four exercises described on the handout; the directions that appear at the top of the handout; the existence of Michael's group; the directions I gave to students to form groups; the introduction I gave to the lesson; the topic of study, namely Indian nationalism; the unit of study, namely South Asia; or the course of study, namely Global Studies. I have learned not to exclude distant points, such as the beginning of the course, in my exercises in backward thinking because, indeed, sometimes that is where the student became lost. For example, if a student says, "Why do we gotta do this stuff, anyway?" it most likely means that he got lost at the beginning of the course, and in that case I must go back to the introductory lesson for the course and rehearse with the student all of the reasons why we gotta do this stuff, anyway. If that is where the student got lost, then a recap of the introductory lesson may work, and the student will go back on task, but very often there are other intervening wrong turns that the student has made since the beginning of the course, so that all of the ground covered between the beginning and the present is utterly unrecognizable. And that's a big problem because it means that really what this student needs is to repeat the course.

However, I don't think Michael became lost at the beginning of the course. After all, he did not say, "Why do we gotta do this stuff?" He said, "I'm lost." When a student

says, "I'm lost," it usually means that he left the trail somewhere during the day's lesson. That puts some helpful limits
on how far back my backward thinking must reach. Time
to ask Michael a question.

"Do you understand the directions on the handout?"

"Yeah, and I got some ideas for number one, but what
I mean is, I don't get what this has to do with anything."

This is a very helpful exchange. From it I learn that
Michael understands the immediate task. Adding this
knowledge to my earlier assumption that Michael was not
lost at the beginning of the course, I figure he became lost
somewhere at the beginning of today's lesson. Time for
another question.

"Do you know who Mohandas Gandhi is?"

"Who?"

Bingo. Alas, while I and some students were discussing
the Gandhi movie, Michael was engaged in some distraction—staring at clock, reading note from friend, writing
note to friend, etching in desk, reading desk, looking at girl
next to him, looking out window, or whatever—and completely missed what I thought was such a marvelously spontaneous introduction to today's lesson.

"Mohandas Gandhi is the person who led the Indian
people to independence from Great Britain. He believed
that the Indians could make the British leave by using nonviolent means. And, believe it or not, he and three hundred
and fifty million Indians did just that. Now, what you are
doing here is imagining you are in the kinds of situations
that Indian people often faced when they were ruled by the
British, and I want you to try to figure out how you could
in some way oppose the British in each of these situations
in some nonviolent manner. Then I'm going to tell you how
Gandhi, himself, did it in each of these situations."

"So I can't shoot anybody, like Gandhi?"

"As with Gandhi, you do not want to harm anyone, right."

"Okay, I get it."

Sweet music to my ears. Pat on the back, Mr. Nehring. Of course, it doesn't always work out that way.

"Yo, dude," Jared calls from the other side of the room. I walk over.

"The name is Nehring, Mr. Nehring."

"Oh, Mr. Nehring."

"Yes, Jared. How may I be of assistance?"

"I am, like, totally lost."

"I see. Well—"

"Will you stop it, Jared!" interrupts Amy, who is sitting next to Jared.

"What? Wha' did I do?" says Jared.

"You kicked me. Mr. Nehring, will you tell Jared to quit kicking me?"

"Jared, stop kicking Amy," I say.

"I didn't touch her. She just wants to get me in trouble."

"Well, I'll tell you what. So that both of you stay out of trouble, why don't we see if we can figure out what you're supposed to be doing with this handout."

"I don't get it," says Amy.

"Why do we gotta do this stuff, anyway?" says Jared.

In my first year of teaching I would have regarded this question as profanity. In my inexperienced teacher's mind I would have interpreted the question to mean, "This stuff is bogus, it's a waste of time," and for anybody to suggest that the lesson I spent three hours preparing the night before, laboring with care to create as an exemplar of instructional technique, is "bogus," and for anyone to suggest that what I spent six years in college and graduate school studying, and which the adult world recognizes without question as important and meaningful, is "a waste of time," well, it just shows what an idiot that person is. Of course, what I did not appreciate in that first year was that it was my job to cure kids of their idiocy, i.e., their self-absorption, by showing them the world has a bearing on their lives.

Anyway, I now take "Why do we gotta learn this stuff, anyway" at face value because it is, after all, a forthright question.

"Jared, what is your ethnic background?"

"My what?"

"Think back to the beginning of the year when I had you do a family tree."

"Oh, yeah. Germany."

"Duh!" says Amy.

"Jared, don't kick Amy. Amy, don't insult Jared. In fact, Amy, do you remember the lesson we did back at the beginning of the year with the family tree?"

"Uh-huh."

"Could you explain to us what Jared's family tree has to do with why we gotta do this stuff?"

"Yes. Back at the beginning of the year we all looked up our family tree. Then we drew a big map at the front of the room and put an *X* where everybody in the class was from. And then we said that the reason that we study other cultures is because everybody in America, except for American Indians, came from other cultures. And if we don't know anything about other cultures, it really means we don't know anything about *our* culture because that's where we're all from, anyway."

"Perfect. I couldn't have said it better. Now, Jared, do you see why we gotta do this stuff?"

"It's boring. I really don't care about all that stuff."

"Jared, do you care about passing this course?"

"Is that a threat?"

"Jared, when I was in high school, I had a teacher who said that there are only two things in life that are required."

"School is one of them, right?"

"No. Death and taxes. You gotta die, and you gotta pay taxes. Everything else is optional."

"So you mean I don't gotta do this stuff?"

"You don't gotta do this stuff. You don't gotta read the paper and know what's going on in the world. You don't gotta pass this course. You don't gotta graduate from high school. You don't gotta get a job."

"Brother . . ."

"I'll be happy to help you if you want help," I say.

"I get it. I'll do it."

If I cannot win their hearts and minds, I may at least win their compliance.

"Who needs help?" Nobody answers. I walk toward Chris, Chrissy, Andrew, Peter, and Naomi, who appear to be hard at work. Andrew and Peter are arguing.

"That's not what Mrs. Hardenburg says."

"Well, maybe Mrs. Hardenburg is wrong."

"Mr. Nehring."

"Yes, Andrew."

"Have you read much Shakespeare?"

"Well, some. And I see a performance now and then."

"Do you think the spirits, elves, fairies, and all are meant to be taken seriously by the audience, or does Shakespeare intend them only as part of the fantasy of the play in general?"

(O goodly students who are thus heterogeneous in thy groups . . .)

40

"Well, I'm not really sure."

"Mrs. Hardenburg says that spirits and elves were part of the medieval worldview, and that Shakespeare probably believed in them and meant them to be taken seriously by the audience."

"Well," I say, "I guess I'm not so sure. Shakespeare was writing in the late 1500s, early 1600s, well into the Renaissance, and given the circles that he would have traveled in, he probably would have been guided by the more rational worldview of Renaissance thinking."

"See," says Peter, "Mrs. Hardenburg is wrong. Any writer living in 1600 who's any good does not go around believing in elves and fairies."

"Of course, I could be all wrong, and maybe Mrs. Hardenburg is right. But tell me, guys, what does this have to do with Mohandas Gandhi?"

"Well . . ." Andrew looks at Peter. Peter looks at Andrew. Andrew says, "We already finished it."

"Let's see." I look over Andrew's handout. It is completely filled out. The answers are creative and show some prior knowledge of the subject. If my slower, less motivated students challenge my skill in backward thinking, students like Andrew and Peter keep me always breathlessly trying to keep astride of a fast-forward pace.

Andrew and Peter are not atypical. There are plenty of intellectually voracious kids who thrive on academia and who challenge their teachers' ability to nurture high-powered, highly motivated intellect. Though they may not be apparent in the chaos of the hallway, they are there between the Walkmans, striding by the huddles of disaffected teenagers, reading quietly in an out-of-the-way alcove, or exploring the library stacks. For them, the system works. They feel challenged in a way that excites them, and they are rewarded with high grades, academic awards, and the approval of their teachers.

Now, having said that Andrew and Peter are not atypical, I am obliged to typify them, but I am not sure I can beyond the fact of their intellectual interests aligning with their academic subjects. And having said that they may be found sequestered in a quiet alcove, I am not sure I want to characterize "them" as out of the mainstream. And having set them apart from a kind of category of intellectual drones who occupy the same heterogeneously grouped class, I want to shatter my all-too-simple categorization and offer what I hope is a more realistic picture.

Andrew's group offers something like a cross section of my ninth-grade class. I'll say what I know about these five students without having done any special research into their family lives or school history.

Here goes: teacher's perceptions of five kids in second-period Global Studies.

Andrew is about five foot four with a head of short, neatly combed light brown hair. His teeth are straight and his fair skin is free of blemishes. His face is still rounded in a childlike way but is fast taking on a mature, hard edge. Andrew's voice is still alto but cracks occasionally. Today Andrew is wearing a blue oxford shirt with button-down collar and a maroon pullover. He has on clean, not-quite-new Levi's jeans and a silver-and-blue pair of Nike running shoes. He carries his books in a yellow Dacron backpack and uses just one strap.

Andrew speaks confidently. His pal, Peter (only the luck of the count-off put them in the same group today), takes his cue from Andrew. Andrew offers a thesis and Peter serves as friendly antagonist in a gentle, egoistic drama that Andrew usually wins or generously concedes to his admiring buddy.

Andrew becomes visibly irritated when his classmates misbehave in class so as to disrupt the lesson. But he does not show irritation at classmates who do not catch on as fast as he does. When someone like Michael asks a "dumb" question, prompting the class to sigh, roll eyes upward, whisper insults, Andrew looks to me with knit brow, as if to say, "My classmates are cruel; I am not cruel." He then looks sympathetically at the student and may even offer a helpful comment.

Andrew serves as a ninth-grade representative to the student senate and is a member of the school swim team.

In class discussions, he usually waits to hear what his classmates have to say, then offers his position—usually moderate and conciliatory—which often becomes a rallying point for further comments by his classmates. His average in my class right now is 94, and I have strong indications that his grades in other classes are equally high.

Peter and Andrew are pals and have been, they tell me, since elementary school. As I've said, Peter takes his cue from Andrew in my class, but I'm not sure that is true elsewhere. Peter is a freer spirit than Andrew, a quality that I think Andrew envies. Today he has on a T-shirt with a silk-screened print of a tuxedo with bow tie. This he complements with a pair of green Army fatigues and well-worn once-white sneakers. Whereas Andrew's thinking is synthetic and conciliatory, Peter's is divergent, antagonistic. Unlike Andrew, Peter is not a clearly recognizable personality in the class. He speaks up only occasionally and is happy to express a divergent point, then let others carry on the discussion without fighting for the supremacy of his idea. He is confident in his views but not compelled to force them on others.

Peter is close to six feet and seems awkward with his tall, gawky frame. His posture is a little hunched, and though confident in his thinking, he is not the leader or organizer that Andrew is.

Peter collects comic books and writes his own cartoon strip, which is unpublished but which he adds to almost every day. I've shown an interest in his cartooning, so he keeps me up-to-date with his main character, a not so mild-mannered punk rocker with orange hair and green teeth who, when called to action over his Walkman head-set, races to the nearest hamburger restaurant and is transformed into a classic American superhero with brilliant white teeth, strong chin, erect posture, and Boy Scout virtue. More than once I've had to gently reproach Peter for cartooning in class. His average in my class is 88. I have a strong feeling that Peter does not work hard to get good grades, and the relatively high scores he does earn come without much effort. But he is by no means docile. He shows intellectual feistiness; it's just that the possibility of high grades does not entice him as it does someone like Chrissy Duncan.

Chrissy's average in this class is currently 98. I mention that first because for Chrissy, high grades and her efforts toward them say much about who she is. She keeps close watch over her average. I've watched her on days that I return a test or assignment. No sooner is the paper in her hand than she has added the grade to a column of numbers and computed its effect on the running score. Like some Wall Street investor reading down the financial page, Chrissy's whole face tenses in anxious anticipation of today's values, as if, like the investor, her net worth should be measured by the daily rise and fall of numerical values.

Chrissy speaks up at least once during each class. She knows I reward class participation. Her comments, though intelligent, are stock. They are lucid, sophisticated, and bland. Her assignments are perfectly done, usually typed on a word processor and printed out in flawless grammar and thorough, clearly organized prose. Her number-two Eberhardt-Faber is always sharp.

Today Chrissy wears a white sweater over a baby-blue turtleneck. She has on tight designer jeans, baby-blue socks to match her top, and clean white tennis shoes. She is a little over five feet with clear fair skin and long blond hair pulled tightly back in a single braid. At fifteen, her tidy frame stands momentarily between girlish and womanly.

Next is Chris James. Chris is a neat dresser, hard worker, and frequent asker of questions. He wants always to be sure that he's following along and doing the right thing. Problem is, he's often not following along, and he's often not doing the right thing—or at least not doing it correctly. Chris has weak comprehension skills and is only marginally literate. His composed appearance and apparent self-confidence are deceptive. He attends remedial classes in addition to his regular academic load and struggles just for passing grades. His current average in social studies is 60. Not passing.

I admire Chris for his unflagging effort despite continual disappointment. But I am concerned that continued frustration in school eventually is going to have to manifest itself somewhere in his life. I tend to think that for Chris this heterogeneously grouped class is not a good idea. In it he sees kids like Andrew and Peter doing well and feeling rewarded. Naturally he compares himself to them and aspires to a level of achievement that is probably beyond his reach.

Finally, Naomi. At the moment Naomi has on her desk Chrissy's paper, which she is copying onto hers. This is group work, they tell me. Naomi has a petite frame and could be mistaken for a boy if not for her hair, which is long, straight, brown, and neatly kept. It is difficult for me to say much about Naomi because, I confess, I don't know much about her. I have not until this moment observed her closely. I think, as a male teacher, I sometimes tend to overlook the girls in my class.

Naomi stands out neither for high grades nor low. She remains inconspicuous by speaking up just often enough to keep me from noting her silence. Her average right now is 75. Average. If she has close friends, they are not in this class because she keeps pretty well to herself. But she's not antisocial. She'll talk and laugh with her classmates if there is a conversation nearby. As with most of my students who earn less than superior grades, I believe Naomi lacks only motivation. (Chris James is an exception to this rule.) But I don't know, or have not yet figured out how to induce excitement for social studies in a slightly immature fifteen-year-old girl—beyond my usual tricks and stunts.

I wonder about the effect of this heterogeneous group on Naomi. It is probably good for her to observe peers who are turned on to the class if, as I assume, what she lacks is motivation. Their motivation may rub off since peer behavior has a strong influence. On the other hand, if Chrissy just gives Naomi the answers, as she did when she handed her the Gandhi handout all filled out, then she's being influenced by the wrong kind of peer behavior.

Anyway, that's Andrew, Peter, Chrissy, Chris, and Naomi. I am trying hard to not typify them, but having described them as individuals, I am prone to circumscribe them as identifiable types of students. My mind is immediately ready with a lot of linear scales along which I can place these individuals. Dull to bright, shy to outgoing, unmotivated to motivated, synthetic to divergent, antagonistic to suppliant, socially immature to mature, and so on. Having observed thousands of students over the years, I find it hard not to make comparisons and arrange categories.

I make one more round of the classroom. Almost everybody is done with the handout—either having written out answers for all of the exercises, run out of ideas, or lost patience and interest. Time to reassemble as a class.

"Please move your chair back to its row," I announce over the din. Slowly some students respond. Michael's group and one other do not. I cup my hands to my mouth, aiming in their direction. "And the teacher said, 'Please move your chair back to its row.' " With some sliding and bumping, a few territorial squabbles, and scattered laughter, the class reassembles approximately in the columns and rows to which they are accustomed.

Looking around the room, I see that everyone has either completed the handout or has gotten about as far as he or she could, which means we're ready to pool our ideas as a class.

"Remember, the purpose of this activity is to introduce you to the nonviolent methods of social change that Mohandas Gandhi used in India. After we've had a chance to discuss the ideas that you came up with for your handout, I will tell you about Gandhi's ideas and some of the situations in which he used them."

This is what teacherdom calls a structuring/directing comment. It tells kids what they're going to do and why they're going to do it. I make a lot of structuring/directing comments because kids need a lot of structuring and directing. Without it the lesson goes haywire; witness my first-year attempt at groups. That went haywire in a big way. Even today I see places in the lesson where a little more structure would have helped. For instance, I did not intend for Naomi to copy Chrissy's work, but given the loose way the groups were set up, it was very easy.

Finding the right balance between not enough structure and too much is in one sense what teaching is all about. Time for one more first-year story. Same low-track class as the other story, only now it's a few weeks later after a classroom ambience of antagonistic chaos has been firmly established. There are regular disturbances—nonstop chatter, verbal assaults, school-kid pranks, and once a fistfight —and I am feeling unable to calm the waters. Truth be told, I am feeling battered by a stormy surf and unable to right myself in the undertow.

So I come up with an idea how to restore control. First I check the supply cabinet in the main office for twenty file folders. Next I write up a list of guidelines for classroom behavior and academic work. The list goes onto a typed sheet, which I staple inside each folder. With my new system students receive two grades each day: behavior and academic. The behavior grade is either 100 or 0—either the kid follows rules and is rewarded or screws up and gets a 0. At the end of class all academic work goes into folder and is graded.

Day one of new program: Students behave and do work according to plan. Everybody gets 100. I envision my forthcoming article in *Social Education*: "How to Reinforce Positive Behavior and Increase Academic Success in the Low-Track Class" by James Nehring, Master Teacher in the Amesley Central School District.

By day five the program has gone to hell.

"Yo, Mr. Nehring, do I still have my hundred for today?"

"Not after that little stunt, Jack. I just wrote your name in the zero column."

"Are you sure?"

"Yes, I'm afraid it's too late."

"Are you like absolutely positive?"

"Yes, Jack."

"Good. Now I can like totally fuck up for the rest of the period and you can't do nothin' about it!"

3.

Discussions

• • •

"Remember, you have a unit test at the end of the week. And you might think, just maybe, about studying for it. Okay, we'll see you tomorrow."

A rush of wind, a shuffle of books, the squeak and bump of forty-odd sneakered feet, and my second-period class jostles toward the door.

"Yo, Matt. I don't think she saw you." Two boys snicker.

"Amy, do you really think Steven could do that?"

"You saw what happened yesterday," says Amy.

A score of conversations sprout from the commotion, some picking up exactly where they left off forty-five minutes ago, some newly begun. The doorway, Venturi-like, sucks up my students while I, now out of the spotlight, collapse unselfconsciously into my chair. I have five minutes until the next class.

"Mr. Nehring, can I have my grades?" From his voice and manner I recognize without looking up that it is Michael, period three, hovering over my collapsed frame.

"No problem, big guy." Automatically I reach for the grade book. "Okay . . ." I muster my dissipated energies and open to Michael's class. "You ready? You have a pencil and some paper so you can write this down?"

"Ah . . . yeah . . . just a minute." Michael searches through his book bag.

"Mr. Nehring!" Amanda, who was just absent from second period, appears at the door. I look up. "Mr. Nehring, I was at the nurse's office. What did I miss?"

"Ahm, well . . ." I begin.

"Okay, I'm ready." It's Michael, pencil and paper in hand.

"Just a second, Amanda. Let me finish with Michael, then I'll give you a hand. Here we go, Michael: 85, 72, 90, 87, 60, 95—"

"Mr. Nehring, can I have the handout from last Tuesday? I was sick, and since the test is at the end of the week—"

"Whoa, whoa. Slow down," I say, interrupting. John, who has entered the room unnoticed, stands squarely, impetuously at my side. "John, I've got two people ahead of you. Please hang on just a minute." John groans impatiently and slaps his hands to his sides.

"Okay, Michael, we left off with 95, right?"

"Yeah."

"Next you have an 80, and finally a 77. You got all that?"

"Yup. Thanks, Mr. Nehring."

"You're welcome." I turn to Amanda. "You're next. Let's see, what did you miss?" I tread water, pondering how to compress a forty-five-minute lesson into a few key words. "Well . . ." I think hopefully, out loud. "Well, no." I change my mind. "It can't be done."

"Whaddaya mean?" Amanda is confused. John continues to harrumph, hands on hips.

"I mean, I simply cannot summarize a whole lesson in thirty seconds. I'll be here this afternoon. If you come by after school, I'll spend as much time as we need to catch you up."

"Great," says Amanda sarcastically, turning to the door.

"You're welcome."

"Next, please." A vision of the long line at the Department of Motor Vehicles flashes across my mind, and I turn to John, who is fidgeting, eyes on the clock. Third period is starting to trickle into the room.

"Mr. Nehring, I'm gonna be late for science," says John.

I look at the clock. "If you stay here, yes, you probably will be."

"Look, all I need is the handout with all the vocabulary."

"Top shelf, back of the room, all the way on the right. Help yourself."

"Thanks."

"Anytime."

"Are we doing anything fun today?" Kathleen, period three, asks the same question she asks every day.

A surge of adrenaline. "Yes. We are doing something so . . . so awesome, so fantastic, you'll just . . . well, you'll just have to wait and see."

"Oh, boy, I'm gonna tell Todd." Kathleen races back into the hallway.

I look at the clock. Two minutes before class is supposed to begin. I need to erase the board from last period; locate my plan, which has disappeared in the paper storm; give a quick look to the absentee list; write a few words on the chalkboard; and go to the bathroom. I start to move quickly, frantically, trying to get everything done. The room fills with third-period students.

"Mr. Nehring, can I go to the bathroom?"

"Yes. Hurry. Go," I command from a cloud of chalk dust, erasing with both hands.

"Mr. Nehring, what are we doing today?"

"We're studying the history of the world," I answer with my face deep in the filing cabinet.

"But we did that yesterday."

"This is the second installment. Everything from the ark forward."

"Oh, that's cool." Fantastically, my answer has satisfied this student's curiosity.

I look at the clock. Time to begin.

"Back. Back, I say!" I brandish an imaginary sword over the students clustered around my desk. They laugh and scatter toward their assigned seats. "Everyone take a seat, please." A commanding appearance belies my own inner feeling of disorientation. I stand before the assembled class and look out over their expectant faces. Four silent questions form in my mind: Which class is this? What am I supposed to teach them? Where am I? When can *I* go to the bathroom?

So the kids are in their seats and I must now forget about going to the bathroom, reengage my brain to nonviolent civil disobedience, and rev up my engines for another lap around the track. The same track. One year I taught nothing but ninth-graders—same course, same ability level, five classes a day, all day long, day in day out, one hundred eighty days in all, count 'em. By the time I reached the third class each day, I experienced déjà vu at frequent intervals. I felt self-conscious telling my bad jokes. When the class groaned, I wondered were they just bad jokes, or were they bad jokes told twice to the same students? Lesson plans, though, were easy. One plan and I was set for the day. In fact, I made some worthwhile improvements on a lot of lessons that year since I wasn't spending my time racing between library, typewriter, and copy machine putting together curricula for three or four different courses. I noticed something also. According to the computer print-out, all five courses were college-preparatory, ninth-grade social studies—GLOBSTU9R, as the computer called them—but in all other respects they were different. Despite our best efforts to heterogenify (whatever) our classes here at Amesley, our kids refused to cooperate.

First period was always submissive and placid no matter how outrageous my props and stunts.

"Now please understand, everyone, I'm showing you this close-up of an old Chinese woman's foot not to gross you out but to help you understand the custom of foot binding, and to make a point." I walk slowly down the rows showing an eight-by-ten black-and-white of a horribly misshapen foot, toes curled under, heel swollen, bone structure all out of line. This is the kind of thing which for most ninth-grade classes will produce exclamations such as "Awesome!" "Sick!" and "Cool!" This morning I can barely coax eyes out of notebooks for a passing glance. Terry cocks his head, grunts, looks down. Kevin checks his watch.

"Foot binding kept a woman's feet small," I say. "Small feet were considered attractive in traditional China." The class stares blankly. "Now, you should write that down because it's important." Twenty-two pens dutifully rise. "Also, you should note that foot binding served to reinforce a male-dominated culture." Jill writes, "F-o-o-t b-i-n-d-i-n-g s-e-r-v-e-d t-o . . ."

I push on. "Now I would like someone to make a guess for us as to how foot binding could serve to reinforce a male-dominated culture."

No takers.

"Well, Amy. Would you like to have your feet bound?"

"I guess not."

"Why not?"

"I don't know."

"Well, what would you have difficulty doing if your feet were bound?"

"I couldn't wear shoes."

"Well, you'd have to wear very little teeny tiny shoes, right?"

"Yeah."

"And your feet would probably hurt, right?"

"I guess."

"And so you wouldn't want to walk around much, right?"

"Whatever."

"And if you can't walk around, you can't go and talk to people and find out who's doing what and when; and you've got to stay home and cook and clean and take care of the kids and basically do what the men tell you, and after all, that's what women are supposed to do, anyway, right?"

"Yeah."

"Yeah? What do you mean 'yeah'?"

"Well, it's what you said."

First period that year reminds me of a story that a science teacher friend tells. He was teaching atomic particles. First he taught about the proton by using a diagram of an atom highlighting the proton. Students listened and wrote. He did likewise with electron and neutron. Finally he showed a diagram with the "crouton," explaining "tasty with salads and soups." Students listened and wrote. The next day he had them correct their notes.

If first-period GLOBSTU9R was submissive and placid, second period was the opposite, proving the point about classes being the same on the computer sheet and very different in reality.

"I'm showing you this close-up photo of an old Chinese woman's foot not to gross you out but to make a point." I show the photo.

"Oh, cool."

"That's gross."

"Wicked."

"Is that her foot?"

"Yup, that's her foot, all right," I say.

"I heard about that once," says Mike.

"What did you hear?"

"How Chinese people bind their feet to make 'em small."

"That's gross," declares Charlie. "I'm sorry, but Chinese people are weird."

"Oooooooohh," goes the class.

"Wait a minute, Charlie," I say. "Back up. Chinese people are weird?"

"I know. I know. It's part of their culture."

"That's right. In Chinese culture, small feet were a mark of beauty."

"It's still weird."

"Is it any weirder than high heels?"

"Yeah. Maybe high heels hurt, but they don't, like, totally mess up your foot."

"So the criterion for weirdness is that something's got to totally mess you up?" I ask.

"Right."

"Dear class, is there anything that we Americans do just for the sake of tradition, or fun or whatever, by which we risk getting totally messed up?"

"Drugs."

"Alcohol."

"Tanning salons."

"Circumcision."

Circumcision? Anyway, first and second periods that year were the same GLOBSTU9R according to the computer, but as different as could be.

The lesson on Gandhi begins again. I ask how one can win a war without putting up a fight, kids offer answers ("Nuke 'em," says Jeff. "Use a tranquilizer gun," says Teige), I explain the handout, and groups go to work. The intro runs smoothly, but I miss the spontaneity of last period's repartee that grew out of my lost lesson plan.

Twenty minutes goes by and I reassemble the mob for discussion.

Discussion. I occasionally read the teacher guides that accompany filmstrips—occasionally because I want to see if what I've thought about filmstrip teacher guides is still really true—that they are most of the time useless. If you don't believe me, look at this.

Acme Associates Presents
The Nigerian Civil War

Instructions:
1. Turn off lights.
2. Tell students they are going to see a filmstrip about the Nigerian Civil War, 1967–1970.
3. Start the filmstrip and tape.
4. At the end of the filmstrip, turn on lights and conduct a discussion based on the filmstrip.

How does one "conduct" a discussion? What is a discussion, such that a person may simply "conduct" one upon turning on the lights? These are important questions, questions that are dealt with in the education courses that teachers universally rail against but the substance of which they rely upon daily. Questions which the people at Acme assume teachers already have a clear and immediate understanding of such that they can instantly "conduct" a discussion upon command in the same manner that they may "turn off lights" and "start the filmstrip." It is all very straightforward, of course.

Not of course. Discussion leading is an art, which a teacher labors daily to master. Back to period three, where the discussion is under way.

"The British hold a monopoly on the production and sale of salt in India. A person may not make or sell salt without the permission of the British government.

"Being an Indian who wants to get the British out of India but who does not want to use violence to get them out, how could you use this situation to your advantage?" Third period's discussion of the Gandhi handout is off and running.

Several hands go up. I consider momentarily the answer I am looking for: mass boycott in which Indians would refuse to buy British-made salt, and acts of civil disobedience wherein so many Indians would illegally make salt that the British jails would not be able to hold all the lawbreakers. I also consider my purpose for holding this discussion: to somehow get my students to give those answers without telling them the answers in advance.

I think about calling on Teige, whose hand is up. He has a loud voice, sits in the back of the room, usually has something thoughtful to say, and will probably get the conversation off to a good start. On the other hand, earlier in the period there was a lot of giggling in Teige's group, which makes me think Teige is looking for laughs today, and whatever he has to say may cause more uproar than debate.

"Frank, why don't you get us started today."

"Well, I say they should either boycott so the British can't make any money and then they'll go out of business, or say to heck with the British laws and just start making your own salt. I mean, they can't go and put a hundred million Indians in jail, right?"

Blaaamm! The answer. I wonder what Acme Associates'

solution is to a discussion short-circuited by a completely correct answer from the first person who speaks.

Frank, I think to myself, you are not playing by the rules. Students aren't supposed to get the answer right away. We're supposed to have some back-and-forth as a class, during which time I coach you toward the right answers and you all slowly see the light. Now there is no suspense.

What to do?

I panic.

"Carey, what do you think of what Frank just said?"

"I don't know, what did Frank just say?"

Bless you, Carey. "Frank, would you please repeat what you just said?" Time to think. It's clear that Frank knows the answer, but there are twenty-three other kids in the room and I have no idea what they're thinking. Happily the discussion may continue.

Frank repeats. Carey says yes, she agrees.

I say, "Well, now, let's all hold on just a minute here. Supposing there is a successful act of civil disobedience, and supposing that, say, fifty thousand Indians participate, the British face a choice about how to react. Meghan, what is the choice?"

"Ahm, well, they can do something or they can do nothing."

"That's right, that's absolutely right. What's the something they could do, Meghan?"

"Put 'em all in jail."

"Right. Now I submit to you that no matter what the British do, they're going to come out the losers in this one. I mean, whether they do something—putting all the Indians in jail, as Meghan suggests—or do nothing, simply ignoring this mass act of civil disobedience, the Indians win. What do I mean? Why do the British stand to lose either way?"

Several hands go up. My confidence is back. The discussion has regained direction. Daniel and Alicia, who sit in the middle of the room, have their hands held high. I almost call on Alicia, but scanning the room, I see that Jason, who rarely says anything, voluntarily or under coercion, doesn't quite have his hand up but is screwing up his mouth and looking in my direction. He needs just a little push.

"Jason, did you want to say something?"

"Well, I'm not sure how to say it."

"Go ahead, give it a shot. We'll be happy to help you out."

"Okay. I think if the British put all the people in jail, then that's gonna make the British look pretty bad."

"Why?"

"Ahm, I don't know."

I decide to not give up on Jason. "Well, Jason, suppose I decide to keep the class after school one day, the whole class, and then I do it the next day, and the day after that. Why do I start to look pretty bad as a teacher?"

" 'Cause you can't control the class."

"Exactly. Now, Jason, why do the British look pretty bad if they put fifty thousand Indians in jail?"

" 'Cause people will say they can't control India."

"Beautiful. You hit the nail on the head, Jason." Jason straightens ever so slightly.

"So, Jason tells us, if the British throw the Indians in jail, the British lose. But what if the British decide to ignore the whole matter? Do they win? Jodi, what do you think?"

"I think they're gonna look like fools because they made a law and now they can't enforce it."

"Yes, I think so too. And if they can't enforce this law, what will the people begin to think about all their other laws?"

"That they can't enforce them, either."

"Yes, so the British lose either way. Now, you may not realize it, but what you have just told me is exactly what Gandhi and his followers did in the 1930s and 1940s."

Now the discussion becomes more a lecture as I take a few minutes to tell the class about the Dandi salt march and Gandhi's numerous boycotts of British goods.

A good discussion is like a good story. If the ending comes too quickly, we say the story is no good because there is no suspense, no drama. But if the ending is obvious, then we say the story is too predictable. Likewise, the storyteller should know the outcome in advance so that everything that comes before somehow leads up to the ending and makes it all the more memorable. Also, a storyteller must know his audience. If the story is too complicated or too simple, all interest will be lost. A good story well told will have a lasting impact upon the listener. A good story you can remember all your life.

Of course, there are those who say that a good story will end without resolution so that the hearer of the tale will be stirred to make up his own ending and thus think critically about the characters and their actions. In this respect, denouement is the enemy. And so it is with some discussions. In GLOBSTU9R, such was the case with a discussion of communism and capitalism.

"Cuba has made great strides since 1959." We are in a unit on Latin America toward the end of the school year. Students are versed by now in the Cold War.

"They're all commies!" Alex calls from the rear of the room.

"Thank you, Alex, for that enlightening comment," I answer. The class laughs. "Yes, that's exactly what they are. Commies. Let's consider what the commies have done in Cuba since 1959. They've taken a country of basically illiterate peasants and after less than thirty years can boast a 96 percent literacy rate. In health care—well, they have about the highest life expectancy of any country in Latin America. Now consider how the commies in Cuba have fared against the non-commies in Haiti—a nearby Caribbean nation that is the economic basket case of the western hemisphere—and you say, 'Hey, maybe these commies aren't so bad, after all.' "

"Whoa, wait a minute, Mr. Nehring. Are you saying communism isn't so bad?"

"Convince me it *is* so bad."

"Well, it's a communist state."

"Yes, that's right," I say.

"They don't have freedom of speech."

"Now you have a point there."

"If it's so great, how come all those people escaped in boats to Miami a few years ago?" A voice from the back of the room.

"I don't know. Good question."

Another voice: "Yeah, and the article you gave us said Castro took control of a billion dollars worth of American companies without paying for them."

"My goodness, that certainly doesn't sound fair," I answer.

"Yeah, and in that article it said almost a million people have escaped since the communist takeover."

"Well, well. That's a lot of people. Class, I'm impressed. You're offering some pretty convincing arguments. I guess what it comes down to is this: Communism, if nothing else, has been relatively successful in improving the standard of living for the average guy in Cuba. On the other hand, in order to do that, they've had to silence anybody who disagreed with their programs so they could move forward as quickly as possible. Now, my question to you is which is the greater right, the right to dissent or the right to a decent standard of living?"

Silence.

The bell rings.

"Have a nice day . . ." I can't resist a little sarcasm.

The class files out.

"Yo, Alex, whaddaya think of the commies now?"

"I don't know. . . ."

"But, Ashley, if everybody has to do what the government says, then I don't care how good their programs are. It's not okay. Freedom is the most important basic right that a person has. . . ."

I am transported to teacher heaven as I catch fragments of conversations that my ninth-grade students—ninth-graders!—are having as they leave the classroom. Discussing political philosophy on their own time. Incredible. Bertolt Brecht said that a play should leave off at the climax, robbing the audience of the catharsis of denouement. That way the audience leaves the theater inventing their own endings and weighing the merits of alternative outcomes. Beautiful.

But my teacherly rapture is cut short. The last comment I make out as students spill into the hallway is, "What the hell is your problem, David? Class is over. The discussion is supposed to end when you walk out the door."

The discussion is supposed to end when you walk out the door. No matter how hard we teachers try to jazz up the course work with innovative activities, "relevant" material, "outside" projects, and "discussions," we have largely failed in what is really our primary mission: to inspire self-learners. The discussion almost always ends at the door.

I remember a diagram I once saw in an education course. Here's what it looks like.

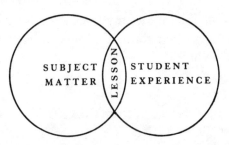

Actually I don't think I ever saw it in an education course, but it sure looks like something one might see on the chalkboard at a teachers' college. I will say I might have seen it in a course, but I might have made it up. At any rate, the key to inspiring self-learners is to find the point at which the student's experience and the subject matter intersect, as in the diagram. That point is the lesson, the beginning of learning, and the means by which the student's realm of experience may be enlarged. It's sometimes difficult to find this point, but you usually know when you've found it. The other day, Tony Desista, science teacher, came into the faculty room and said, "You know, my tenth-graders are real pissers this year. For the last month I have been on the verge of giving up on them. Nothing excites them. But today we were doing the brain; you know, all the different lobes and what the function of each one is, etc., etc. Anyway, they were really getting into it. Apparently there's a TV cartoon about somebody's brain, and there are all these little animated characters that race around this factory that's supposed to represent different parts of the brain. It was great. We really connected."

Tony evidently found the point of intersection.

Today's lesson on Gandhi is an attempt to exploit this point of intersection. I create an historical moment and place the kids in it. I ask, What would you do? And then I tell them this is what the famous person Gandhi did. And the students say (I hope), Gee, that's interesting, because now they have the basis for a comparison of Gandhi's actions within their own experience.

All this looks great on paper, but in real life, great discussions, in which the teacher finds that elusive point of intersection between student experience and course curriculum, don't always happen. In fact, a good part of the time they don't happen.

It's mid-November and we're deep into Chinese history. The temperature in the room, as is customary for days that are below freezing outdoors, hovers around eighty degrees. The seats are draped with twenty-six students, all at varying degrees of inclination to the floor. Duane rolls his eyes. Alfred's tongue lolls. Mary's head is nestled comfortably between arms folded on desktop.

"The dynastic cycles of Chinese history bear out the viability of the Chinese concept of the Mandate of Heaven as a measure of public confidence in the emperor."

Another head drifts quietly to the surface of another desk.

"The Ch'in Dynasty, short-lived but significant for its implementation of the philosophy of legalism as a system of government, ended in a popular uprising that gave birth to the Han Dynasty—the new bearer of the Mandate of Heaven, and a highly successful dynasty that ruled China for centuries."

Whenever I sense that I'm losing my students, my sentences start to get long-winded and I begin to hear myself talk. The words just kind of mindlessly rush along from well-worn scripts in the yellowed lecture-note portion of my brain, wander about the room in the spaces between student desks, and, seeing that no one is taking any interest, pass through the louvered vent in the door and dissipate into the emptiness of the hallway.

"Oh, my God, Mr. Nehring, I'm about to croak!" Kimberley

Neill, plunk in the middle of the room, plastered against the back of her chair, arms thrown back, cries in anguish.

"What's the matter, Kim?"

"This lecture is *so incredibly boring!*"

A lecture is not a discussion. In a lecture one person talks. In a discussion there is back-and-forth. If one person talks, the action in the classroom is fairly predictable and therefore easily gets boring. But if two or more people are carrying on a conversation, a drama unfolds. Even if the destination is known, the passage is uncertain and exciting. That is why I have to laugh when I read directions such as, "Turn off filmstrip projector. Conduct a discussion." A good discussion is never mechanical. And a masterful discussion calls for skillful judgment and some very fast decision making.

Decisions. In addition to everything else, a good discussion involves a lot of fast decisions by the person who leads it. In fact, a good discussion calls for more decisions than I could count. I know because I tried counting them once. Actually I decided I would try to chronicle all the decisions I made in the course of a half-period discussion. I soon found that even that modest goal was too ambitious. I got as far as a half minute. I counted twelve decisions in all. If this is a typical half minute, then, figuring that I spend about six hours with students in a day, that's 8,640 decisions per day.

Back to period three and Mohandas Gandhi. The period is almost over.

"Mr. Nehring, did you see the TV show last night about nuclear protests?"

"Well, no, Jodi. Does it have something to do with Mohandas Gandhi and civil disobedience?"

"Kind of . . ."

A dilemma. Jodi is a great provocateur of The Digression, which in school lingo means any class discussion students believe is a departure from the teacher's plan but which the teacher has enough interest in to tolerate. There are some students who scheme digressions—Jodi is one—and, when the moment is right, will launch an opening salvo: Did you see the TV show? You wanna know something interesting my father told me last night? You know, I saw this movie once. . . . If I give Jodi the go-ahead, I lose control of the discussion. If I stop her in her tracks, then she'll put on a sullen face and the whole class could turn sour. Either way there is potential risk and gain. Of course, losing control of the discussion is not necessarily a bad thing. When kids control the discussion, they sooner or later wind up talking about themselves. When they talk about themselves, they show me who they are—useful stuff for a teacher. On the other hand, if I've got something in mind for my students to learn and they're running the discussion, chances are they won't learn it.

What to do? We've pretty well brought into the open all the strategies of Gandhi's campaign that I wanted my students to be versed in. Everyone's had a chance to throw in his two cents. We have only a few minutes left in the period, anyway. And Jodi is an adorable schemer. What the hell.

"Go ahead, Jodi."

"Well, there was this show last night, and it was all about why we shouldn't have nuclear power plants."

"Oh, yeah. I saw that," says Bob.

"Anyway, they showed how if there's an accident, the whole planet can blow up and spread all this radioactivity all over the place. And they said how most places where they have nuclear plants don't have good evacuation plans. And besides, I mean, do you really think people are gonna listen to some plan if there really is an accident?"

"I think all that stuff is bogus," says Marc.

"It is not," Jodi insists.

"Come on, they have so many safety checks at those places, and they've got government people inspecting all the time. The chance of anything happening is like incredibly, incredibly small."

"Yeah, but what if something does happen?" The class seems to be with Jodi on this one.

Marc answers. "Well, those are the chances you gotta take. Hey, everything's risky. You cross the street, you could get hit by a truck."

"Yeah, but come on, Marc, this is a little different."

"I think they all don't care, anyway." This is Nicole. "I mean, all the big leaders are all like sixty and seventy years old and they know they aren't gonna be around in twenty years. So whatta they care if the world gets messed up?"

From the front row: "Yeah, ya know, whenever there's a war, it's always the young people that go and fight and the old farts stay home and let all the kids get killed."

"You know, when I grow up, I'm gonna move out to Montana and build a log cabin and live off the land," says Jodi.

"Hah, that's a laugh," says Marc. "What are ya gonna do when you wanna watch TV?"

"I won't watch TV."

"Huh, like I really believe that."

"I think the kids should take over the country." Another voice from the back of the room.

"I think it's all hopeless, anyway."

"Hey, Mr. Nehring, what do you think if we used some of this nonviolent stuff to protest?"

"I don't know. What do you think? What are you gonna protest?"

"The smoking area. They should make it indoors."

"Yeah" comes from all corners of the room.

"Or passes. We should get rid of passes."

More yeahs.

"I think we should boycott the cafeteria."

"I think we should boycott classes."

"I think we—"

The bell rings.

Class files out.

"Yo, Marc, what are you doing after school?"

"Hey, I hear Amy's got a new VCR."

"Have you seen the Madonna video?"

"After school, you wanna go to the mall?"

4.

The Disciplined Mind

• • •

It takes about two minutes to walk from my classroom to the In-school Suspension Room where I serve as supervisor during fourth period. If I am not engulfed by students with questions at the end of third period, then I can gather up my books, papers, pencil, pen, etc., and lock up the room in about a minute. That means if all goes without interruptions or delay, I am at the ISS Room two minutes before period four begins. Close tolerance is critical since Bill Pierce, who covers ISS during third period, waits for me each day and needs at least two minutes to race from ISS to his classroom and get settled. Out of fairness to Bill, I hustle out of Room 25 every day after my second round of GLOBSTU9R and hightail it to ISS. Every day I arrive breathless, and Bill departs anxious. Today, however, as I approach, Bill is not standing, as he usually does, at the ISS door. Indeed, as I step through the doorway I see that Bill is not in the room. There is no teacher in the room. And all hell has broken loose.

But first I will tell you what ISS is all about. In-school suspension became popular in the 1970s as an alternative to out-of-school suspension (OSS). Instead of rounding up the smokers, vandals, bullies, and troublemakers and kicking them out of school for a day or a week, school officials decided they would place the school's social miscreants in a kind of holding tank/isolation box within the school building for the same amount of time. Thus it used to be if Johnny screwed up, the vice principal would say, "Now, Johnny, if you screw up again, you'll be suspended for five days." Willy-nilly, you can bet, Johnny screwed up and won himself five days off from school. But with the advent of ISS, the vice principal could say, "Johnny, if you screw up, it's into the slammer." And Johnny would think maybe he'd better not screw up.

If ISS was popular among school folks for its threat value, it was also embraced as a way of maintaining control. In the days of OSS, troubled kids would be turned over to empty homes of working parents or, worse yet, to parents who were alcoholic and abusive. In any case, the school had no control over a kid's OSS experience. But it did have control with ISS. ISS meant the school had an opportunity to engage in some kind of rehabilitation effort while the kid was serving out his term.

Opportunity. Prison is an opportunity, an opportunity for society to create a positive environment to reshape lives that have been misshaped by a rotten environment. We're not supposed to call prisons prisons; officially they're correctional facilities. But everybody knows they do not correct, and so we call them prisons. They do not offer the positive environment they should. They are a missed opportunity.

"Oh, shit!" Jason Rosenblum, who has been riffling through the supervisor's desk drawers, looks up and sees me standing in the doorway. He hustles off to his seat. Meanwhile Eddie Hastings is standing on the counter at the front of the room monkeying with the wall clock.

"Yo, Eddie," Jason calls in stage whisper.

"Yeah, what?" He doesn't turn around, which means he doesn't see me. I say nothing.

"Ah . . . Eddie . . ." says Jason.

Eddie turns around. "Hey, Mr., ah . . ."

"Nehring," I say.

"Yeah, Mr. Nehring. Like, I was just fixin' the clock."

"I see."

Eddie climbs down from the counter.

"Where's Mr. Pierce?" I ask.

"He booked," says Jason.

"Well, usually he books after I arrive. Anybody know why he booked early?" I look around the room.

Says Jason, "Don't know, dude. Just booked, that's all."

Recently Ralph Peters sent out a memo.

MEMO

To: Faculty

From: Mr. Peters

Re: Punctuality and Supervisory Duties

        Please remember that the effective operation of our school depends on the cooperation of everybody. Punctuality for supervisory duty is essential to the smooth running of the school. Please cover your duty for the full time assigned. Thank you for your anticipated cooperation.

Punctuality is well and good, but in the frantic reality of a teacher's day it becomes a kind of a quaint concept. Bill Pierce, and all the teachers whose absence from duty must have prompted the principal's missive, no doubt had good reason for going AWOL: copy student handouts, set up VCR, run errand to guidance office, accompany sick kid to nurse, accompany unruly kid to main office, replace burnt-out projector bulb, go to bathroom, and so on. I don't blame Bill.

Nonetheless, sympathy for Bill Pierce does not help restore order to the small (fifteen by fifteen), windowless,
sweltering ISS room, which today is packed to capacity
with nine of Amesley's toughest cases. Eddie is now off the
counter and browsing around the front of the room. Jason
and two other boys whose names I don't know are pacing
up and down the side of the room. Another boy, who looks
like about an eighth-grader, is making fart noises with
cupped hands at his desk. Another youngish-looking boy
sits just in front of him, attempting to do the same by
cupping his left hand in his right armpit, but he's not suc-
ceeding and looks discouraged. Two other boys, maybe
fifteen or sixteen, sit side by side wide-eyed over a magazine
centerfold of a pickup truck with ridiculously oversize tires
driving ably over a lineup of crushed passenger cars. At the
center of the room, serving as a kind of motionless hub
about which this stormy cosmos of teenage wildness spins,
sits enormous Belinda Ballou, calmly completing French
workbook exercises.

What to do? Restore order. How?

My gut reaction is to make some big, voicy command,
march about sternly thrusting my arms in the air, and,
with an immense samurai look of menace, glare my unruly charges into their seats and silent submission. But
I've never been real good at that. I know teachers who are.
Sarge Engstrom, retired Navy man who saw teaching as
a logical second career after thirty-one years of military
duty, ran his classroom as everyone imagines boot camp
to be. He was fond of slamming a meter stick on his desk
to get attention. If a student dared to fall asleep during
reminiscences of Korea, Sarge blew a whistle in his ear.
But the ultimate intimidation tactic was reserved for Jim
Johnson, whose reputation for troublemaking preceded
him into the ninth grade and who Sarge kept after class on

the first day of school. Sarge told me the story more than once.

"Stick around, Johnson." Rest of class files out. Sarge closes door.

"Listen, Johnson. This year you aren't gonna screw around in class, right?"

"Yes, Mr. Engstrom."

"This year you and me are gonna play ball, right?"

"Yes, sir."

"And do you know why, Johnson?"

"Ah, no."

"Because if you don't play ball with me, I'm gonna ram the fucking bat up your ass."

Just make sure if you rough a kid up, Sarge would tell me, there are no witnesses. Hey, it's the only way you can reach some of these kids, Sarge would say.

I tried (just once) to copy Sarge, but when my meter stick broke and all my students laughed, I decided fear and intimidation were not my strong suits.

That leaves reason and maybe humor.

I walk over to Jason Rosenblum. "Jason, have a seat, please"

"*Ee-yo*, dude, Mis-ter Nay-Ring."

"Jason, I think it would be a good idea for your own sake to have a seat."

"Whoa, like I'm scared."

"Jason, I'm not trying to scare you. I just don't want you to get in any more trouble. Besides, we don't keep the passes in the desk."

Jason stops short. "Oh. Well, okay, that's cool." Jason sits. "The rest of you guys want to have a seat, please?"

Seeing that Jason is down, the rest of the group figures they may as well do likewise.

Calming down a noisy, rebellious group of adolescents is

a lot like defusing a bomb. Careful, premeditated, calm responses are crucial to success. Overreact and the thing explodes in your face. A bomb does not explode by accident. There are reasons. Somebody sets it ticking, the breeze blows a certain way. Wires get crossed. Unless the bomb squad has some respect for the device in question, they will not long be a bomb squad. An amateur does not appreciate this. He just sees the bomb and figures he has to stop it. Chuck it out the window. Throw a blanket over it. Unacquainted observer walks into ISS room, sees kids running around, riffling through desk, tearing clock off wall, general chaos. Thinks, Got to stop it. Open the window. Get a blanket.

So everybody's in his seat, anyway. Preparedness Alert may be reduced one danger level. I sit at the supervisor's desk.

"Do you guys all have work to do?"

A few grunts, mostly no response. That's okay, I asked more to let everyone know I'm taking an interest than to get any substantial information. I locate a bunch of assignment sheets in the top left drawer.

ISS ASSIGNMENT

Student: ___Billy Lieber_____

Teacher: _____Mrs. Burke_____

Assignment: __Read pp. 221–234—do_____

_____exercises._____

"Billy Lieber?" I look around the room.

"Yo," says a kid in the front row.

"Billy, what are you doing?"

"He's pickin' his nose," says another kid in the front row.

"Yeah, pretty soon he ain't gonna have no brain left," says another. I figure I can ignore the comment, in which case they'll know they're bugging me. Or I can say something like, "He's still got more brains than you" (what I'd really like to say), but then I'm playing bully, too, and that gets us nowhere. Or I could chuckle just a little and they'll see the teacher has a sense of humor and maybe calm down some, but that won't help Billy Lieber any.

"Are you guys always so considerate?" is what I finally say, and the two kids give a nervous laugh and go back to their business. Billy looks up, feeling a little vindicated.

"Billy, what are you doing?" I repeat.

"Nothin'."

"Well, did you know you have an assignment here from Mrs. Burke?"

"I did it already."

"Where is it?"

"Ah, I think I got it in my notebook here." Billy sets to looking in his notebook.

"Robbie Blankenship?" I call. No answer.

"Is Robbie Blankenship here?"

"Yes! Yes! I said yes!" says Robbie.

"I have three assignments here, all with your name on 'em."

"I know," says Robbie. "I got three here too. I'm doin' em."

"Good. Very good." I begin to feel like there's something of an academic mood settling over the group.

"Keep your fuckin' hands offa me, kid!" Belinda Ballou explodes, and the frustrated, would-be maker of fart noises flies slam against the wall. I imagine stars above his head. He tries to gather himself up off the floor. He is definitely shaken.

"Whoa!" I rise, thinking stupidly that doing so will forestall continued violence.

"Whoa!" I repeat, not quite sure what else to say.

What else to say? "Are you okay?" I approach the hapless victim, who certifies that he's a-okay. I look over at Belinda, who has returned to French workbook exercises.

"Excuse me, Miss Ballou." Teachers always go for the *mister* or *miss* when there's trouble. Belinda keeps on with the workbook, only now she looks a little more intent.

"Ah, Miss Ballou. You just struck this person here." The obvious seems worth stating.

"Belinda, did you hear me?" By the look on her face I can tell Belinda is beginning to feel committed to the idea of giving me the silent treatment.

"What has just happened here is definitely not okay," I think aloud. "Kid A strikes kid B . . . with serious degree of force. Supervising teacher should call main office to request assistance from school administrator." I walk over to the intercom by the desk.

"He hit me first," says Belinda finally.

I stop and turn.

"Yes, but you didn't go flying against the wall and smash your head," I answer, and turn to the victim. "What is your name, son?"

"Mike Robard."

"Mike, did you hit Belinda?"

"I was just foolin' around."

"Yeah, right, just foolin' around," says Belinda. "You guys are always makin' fun of me and I've had about as much as I can take."

"Mike, do you feel all right? Do you want me to call the nurse?"

"I'm okay."

"Do you have work to do?"

"Yeah, I got work."

"Good. Do it. And Mike, don't touch Belinda. Belinda,

don't touch Mike." I push the intercom to talk. "Ah, this is Jim Nehring in ISS."

"Yes, Mr. Nehring."

"We just had an altercation here between Belinda Ballou and Mike Robard. Everything seems to be under control at the moment, but maybe you could ask Mr. Handelman to swing by when he has a minute."

"Thank you, Mr. Nehring. I'll tell Mr. Handelman."

The invocation of the vice principal's name seems to have had a silencing effect on the group. Six out of nine are into their books. Billy Lieber is still trying to make a good show of looking for the missing assignment. I rise. Walk over to Billy.

"Any luck?" I ask.

"I know I did it." Should I tell him to do it again? He might make a big scene. And that could get the rest of the group in an uproar, and pretty soon I'd have kids ripping clocks off walls again. No, a big scene is not a good idea. "Tell you what. Why don't you work on something else and we'll see if it turns up later."

"Okay."

I walk back to my desk.

Why not a big scene? Because then the group would be out of control. So? So ISS is supposed to be a punishment; if the kids are having a great time ripping clocks down, then it's not a punishment. Important to keep the lid on. But if you keep the lid on, it means the pressure doesn't escape. If the pressure doesn't escape, then maybe you have an explosion. And if you have an explosion, then the kids get in trouble. And then what do you do? You send them to ISS.

"Hey, man, can we like open the door? It's boilin' in here."

"Well, if I open the door, will you promise to not be distracted by whatever's going on in the hall?"

"Yes," everybody promises together.

"Okay, as long as everybody's doing what they're supposed to, the door stays open." I pull the door open. Swing it back against the wall. I have just made a threat. Which I am able to enforce. I seem to recall from my upbringing or some education course or other that that's the correct kind of threat to make. Don't make idle threats. Always be sure you can carry it out. Truly I can carry out this threat. I can close the door. Okay, you guys, I said if you fooled around, I'd close the door. I wish I didn't have to, but I have no choice. When carrying out a threat, always make sure that responsibility for the consequences is clearly established. Of course, if I carry out this threat, I, too, have to live with the consequences, which in this particular instance means sweltering in an overheated isolation chamber with nine ornery adolescents who in addition to being ornery are now sweating too.

So what does this fifteen-by-fifteen rehabilitative center look like, anyway? Besides being square, it is oppressively windowless, an oppressiveness that is compounded by the construction material for the walls: cinder block, except for the doorway to the hall (and another sealed doorway leading to who knows where). The door itself is thick and made, I think, of aluminum, comparing favorably with the kinds of doors found on walk-in freezers in butcher shops such that when the door is shut, the room resounds with a kind of terminal *ka-chung*. Last summer, somebody on the custodial staff painted those cinder blocks with a heavy coat of light blue glossy latex. Mr. Peters remarked that this was his idea, as the color blue is "psychologically calming"—his words. (I try to imagine what the kids would be like in here without the benefit of Mr. Peters's blue walls.) Entering the room from the hallway, the supervisor's wooden desk is to the right. Nine welded desk and chair units are arranged in three rows, facing away from the door. The wall that students get to stare at all day at the far end of the room is plastered with:

Rules and Regulations for ISS

1. You are responsible for your own actions.
2. Complete all work assigned.
3. No talking or food of any kind.
4. You may go to the bathroom once in the morning and once in the afternoon.

Let's take rule one, which is not really a rule, but no matter. I have yet to meet a high-school kid who looks ahead, in advance of acting, to the consequences of his actions. There is something about the adolescent mind that blocks out all apprehension of causal relationships.

"Johnny, you failed for the quarter."

"Whaddaya mean, I failed? How come?"

"Well, because you did not turn in ten out of twenty assignments."

"But what about the ones I did?"

"The ones you did were just fine. It's the ones you didn't do that made you fail."

"That's unfair. You can't count that against me just 'cause I didn't do 'em."

The dysfunction is greatly frustrating for adults who work with adolescents day in and day out, continually foreseeing the consequences, usually ill, of Johnny's or Amy's willful self-destruction but powerless to share the vision of doom with the soon-to-be-affected party. It's enough to make a perfectly sane adult want to print at the front of every classroom in America, "You are responsible for your own actions." But nobody would read it. And even if somebody did, it wouldn't make no sense no how. We humans seem to have to get burned, usually more than once, before we get the idea that red coils really do mean HOT STOVE.

Some years ago a kid at Amesley committed suicide. On a Saturday afternoon in April, Tanya, a senior, left her house to take the dog for a walk. A few hours later the dog came back without Tanya. The leash was missing. Her mother found Tanya suspended from the swing set at the elementary school where a little while earlier she had hanged herself with the dog's leash. The community was shaken by Tanya's death. In the schools, teachers and students attended seminars on stress and teen suicide. We conducted a thorough review of school support services and participated in workshops to develop sensitivity to signs of emotional stress in our students. Those were all good things to do, but they're not what I most remember about the tragedy. A few weeks after Tanya's death a teacher made a comment in a faculty-room discussion. Conversation had turned somber and reflective. "Maybe she really didn't think it would work," he said. "Maybe she just thought she'd try it . . . just to see what would happen."

Amazingly most of us make it through adolescence more or less intact while having learned something about hot stoves.

And so there, against the blue wall of ISS, stands Rule and Regulation Number One, firmly affixed within the environment if not the minds of today's nine students.

"This sucks. Can I go to the bathroom?" It's Allen, I see from the seating chart I've just located, lover of pickup trucks with big tires. When I was in eighth grade, *suck* was a heavy word reserved for occasions of high drama when nothing but deep vulgarity would do: "You turned me in for spray-painting the boys' bathroom. You suck." Something like that. But like another word we've already talked about, it seems to have lost some of its emotive force over the years. If *fuck* and *suck* no longer impress people as mean and abusive, then what's left? Could this be the end of verbal abuse in the English language? Have we reached a linguistic dead end? We'll think of something.

"Go ahead." Allen "books."

George Handelman arrives. Stands in the doorway.

"Hello, Mr. Nehring."

"Hello, Mr. Handelman." This being a formal visit, George and Jim follow formal visit protocol. Lots of Mr. this and Mr. that.

"I understand there was an altercation here."

All eight students busy themselves with work that has appeared from nowhere. Belinda Ballou is heavily into French workbook exercises, volume two.

"Yes. You might wish to speak with the two persons involved." I point.

"Miss Ballou, could I see you in the hall for a minute?"

Belinda wriggles free of her chair and desk. She's big enough that it takes some effort. Everybody looks. Belinda holds her chin up. Walks out. Door closes. *Ka-chung.*

Inside, we all pass a minute in silence, partly because the kids are afraid of Mr. Handelman and partly because we all are dying to know what's being said on the other side of that all-too-well-insulated metal door.

Door opens. Belinda enters. Sits. More French workbook.

"Mr. Robard?" George beckons.

Mike rises solemnly, head bowed ever so slightly. *Ka-chung.* Again the silent minute. Again the door opens. Mike takes his seat.

"Ah, Mr. Nehring. Miss Ballou and Mr. Robard will be

with you another day. I'd say everything here looks pretty shipshape."

"Right-o, Mr. Handelman," I say. "Thanks for stopping by."

Ka-chung.

Schools place a premium on everything shipshape. Which is to say everything's gotta look orderly. That's the priority. No gum. Columns and rows. No writing on the desks. Everyone sitting up straight, looking busy. No talking. Shipshape.

Throw a blanket over it.

Ten minutes pass. Allen returns.

"Where've you been for the last fifteen minutes?" I ask.

"The bathroom upstairs was locked. I had to go down by the gym."

Allen sits. I don't bother to question further. Neither do I doubt his story. Kids are always leaving my classroom to go to the bathroom, returning late, and claiming the bathroom is locked. The story usually checks out. So why is the bathroom locked? one might reasonably ask. So, of course, the kids can't vandalize it is the answer. But neither can they use it for that purpose for which the bathroom was intended, one might logically point out. The locked bathroom is a kind of archetypal school phenomenon, archetypal in that it lays bare the essential logic of the institution, a logic that informs all other activities but in the case of the bathroom is especially transparent.

Since Ralph and George have been cracking down lately on underage smokers in the designated student smoking area, dissidents have sought refuge in the only other readily accessible place at Amesley that affords some privacy. And between classes, or during classes by way of excuse to go to the nurse to get my inhaler or find my pocketbook, which I think I left in science, those not old enough to torment their lungs legally head to the nearest john and light up. Recently the boys' room across the hall from Ethel Port, who teaches film and lit, lit and society, fantasy lit, and all other lits, available mainly to seniors, has been particularly smoky. Ethel, who is fifty-one days from retirement, is on a crusade. Maybe because she is fifty-one days from retirement she feels intensely a compulsion to straighten kids out in a way she has not been able to in the forty-odd years she has been at Amesley. A kind of urgency about the Moral Education of Youth. So it is that Miss Port has been seen lecturing tough-looking suspected smokers about death at a young age, the chain-smoking aunt who died not long ago of emphysema, and the (fictitious) lawsuit being brought against the school by a parent whose kid can't go to the bathroom because the bathrooms are so full of smoke and he's got asthma. Actually Ethel's lectures are like some childish display of name-calling, as the kid who happens to be Ethel's target ignores Miss Port's advance, starts walking the other way down the hall, and Miss Port starts calling after him about death at a young age and the aunt and the lawsuit, and as the kid puts more distance between himself and Miss Port, Ethel just calls louder and louder, and pretty soon Miss Port's just yelling at the end of the hall because the kid has disappeared around the corner, but Ethel, crusader that she is, won't give up.

Under the weight of police-type crackdowns by Mr. Peters and Mr. Handelman, as well as the force of Miss Port's lectures, the kids have begun to show remarkable signs of ingenuity. In fact, like survivors of Nazi concentration camps and Soviet gulags, these kids have turned the circumstances of their oppression into a kind of game. I first became aware of this when one day between classes, whilst I was directing traffic in the halls and listening to excuses about how someone's mother overslept so he didn't get the assignment done, Ethel came bustling over from her own post in front of her room (across from the boys' bathroom) and asked if I couldn't run into the bathroom for just a moment because there were some boys smoking in there, and if they all saw Ethel coming, the guards at the door would give the high sign to the kids inside, and by the time Miss Port had entered the bathroom (which she did regularly) and bustled down to the last stall on the right where all the incriminating smoke was just pouring out from above and below, those cigarettes would be out cold and the kid would say, see the cigarette's out cold, or the toilet would flush and all that great evidence would be neatly, permanently down the drain.

More out of curiosity than any sense of urgency about catching smokers, I obliged Ethel and headed for the bathroom. After all, guards at the door? This was something worth seeing. Sure enough, as soon as Mr. Nehring came into view near the bathroom door, some big kid with a wool cap hollered into the boys' room something like, "Narc at twelve o'clock" or some such phrase, and by the time I was to the urinals, all those suspicious-looking underage troublemaker-type kids were saying, "Ain't no cigarettes here, man," and I looked like an idiot and the kids felt great because they'd won this round. And I could tell they were all just hoping Miss Port would be waiting outside so they could disappear around the corner while she was at full throttle about the sick aunt and death at an early age.

Pretty soon it became clear that the kids were winning more than an occasional battle. So someone—and it's not clear to me whether it was Ralph Peters, George Handelman, or one of the custodians (they are the only ones with keys to such important places as the boys' bathroom)—locked the door. The lines of commitment deepened along the brows of all those professional troublemakers when they went to kick open the bathroom door in a customary manner before homeroom and it wouldn't budge. This means war, those furrowed brows said. Then, in homeroom, the conversation was all about the boys' room and how are we supposed to go to the bathroom and isn't that illegal, and why punish everybody for what a few kids do.

As for my classes, this latest development meant that whenever a boy had to go to the bathroom, instead of heading out the door and walking about twenty paces down the hall, the kid had to go all the way down the hall, down the stairs to the first floor, down one long corridor and around the corner to the next nearest boys' room. All in all, this added a good five minutes to a bathroom foray and meant the kid would miss a good ten minutes of class. And of course, upon returning, there would have to be an explanation of how the boys' room upstairs was locked and how he had to go to the one downstairs. And then Mr. Nehring would say it's okay, he understands, and then everybody else would start in about how are we supposed to go to the bathroom and isn't that illegal, and why punish everybody, and still more time would be lost from whatever it was we were supposed to be doing in class.

Back in ISS everyone seems to have settled down to some activity or other. Allen is busy cracking his knuckles, feeling relieved from his one allowable morning pit stop (and probably a good smoke in the boys' bathroom). Billy Lieber has gone back to looking for his (probably nonexistent) missing assignment. Belinda continues to plow through volume two. Eddie is staring at the clock, no doubt looking for that hidden service screw that'll free the whole thing—face, casing, and all—from its anchor on the wall. Robbie is buried nose-deep in Allen's pickup truck magazine and everybody else is more or less upright at his desk, in the right row and column, involved in some pretense or other of school-sanctioned activity. Thus we ride out the rest of fourth period together, me and my socially maladjusted youths who by virtue of their ISS confinement are clearly on their way to rehabilitation and reform.

I remember a philosophy of education course. The topic of the week was discipline. What is the nature of discipline? or some such. Professor Arnold was quite a master of Socratic dialogue. With careful maneuvering he led us future educators of America out from the mire of ignorance into the full light of the word's true meaning. Discipline. The discussion had started out predictably, about kids being on task on time in their seats, following bells, having sharpened pencils, doing homework, raising hands, no gum, no talking. Then we started reading some of the big shots like John Dewey and Alfred North Whitehead and all the rest and we commenced arguing among ourselves about the true nature of discipline and gradually started to develop something of a consensus (old Professor Arnold started to crack a kind of a wry smile at this point, like he had no idea how we all came to this consensus) that discipline had little to do with externals like hand raising and running in the halls but was really an interior quality, a habit of mind, a devotion to work, an internally driven commitment to the goodness, rightness, and urgency of some project such that one will work. Hard. So we all agreed: Sure, that was it. And then we went on and took our masters degrees and started teaching school and over the course of time and five classes a day and a hundred and fifty kids and five minutes between classes and fuck you and papers to correct and kids snapping gum and ripping down clocks and keeping order in the halls and let's just try to keep the lid on in ISS and shipshape, we forgot the true meaning of discipline.

One summer I painted the back porch. Being so exposed to the elements, it had come to look considerably shabbier than the rest of the house, which was already generally pretty shabby-looking, anyway. Prior to commencing, I had heard plenty of good advice about scraping off the old paint so there's no peeling, and filling those exposed nail holes to keep rust from bleeding out, and washing off the mildew, and replacing the rotted boards and so on. But being by nature impatient with such tedious tasks as painting porches, I went for the quick fix. (Throw a blanket over it.) On went that gallon of latex semigloss, applied with a good wide brush so as to speed things up, and in no time that old shabby porch looked just grand. And how everybody remarked all through the summer at outdoor barbecues about how good the porch looked.

The next March, as the last patches of snow lay melting around the corners of the porch, I noticed that there was mildew growing up right where it used to be on the edges of the floor slats. And around the steps where it had once been peeling, that new latex semigloss was ever so subtly starting to lift away from the surface of the wood and up around the rail that had been showing some signs of rot. The new paint was bubbling up. Stubborn and impatient, I dug up the leftover latex and slopped on a good heavy layer over the affected areas. Treat the symptoms is what the medical profession always says, and why should painting be any different? All summer long I treated those symptoms, but that peeling, rotting, bubbling porch did not catch on. Finally, on advice of a professional painter friend whose advice I really did not need to tell me what I already knew but simply did not have the patience to accept, I decided to do it the right way. The next summer, I scraped down the porch, scrubbed away the mildew, filled in the nail holes, replaced the rot, primed, and then painted. It took all summer, and barbecue guests did not remark about how great the porch looked, but that was okay because I knew

I was doing it right, and when you do things right, they often look a mess but that's only because they're being done the right way, and after all, there's serious work in progress here and so who cares what it looks like right now. Well, finally the porch was fixed. Right.

Teachers should not look to doctors for advice about how to educate the young.

A closing story.

One Friday night, Mr. Nehring, accompanied by Mrs. Nehring, went to the mall. For a teacher, going to the mall is always an adventure fraught with the possibilities of both happy and hazardous encounters and loaded with surprise. For the mall, especially on a Friday night, is loaded with kids, and the mall is clearly their turf. Here they may smoke in public without a teacher saying no, they can't. Here they may swear and make obscene gestures while the anonymous public pays them no mind. In fact, the anonymous public will make wide detours around groups of swearing, obscene, gesturing, smoking teenagers for fear those teenagers may verbally accost them, calling them square grown-ups and laughing at their square clothing (even though the group is probably too self-absorbed to notice the square-looking adults, anyway). On a Friday night the kids are out, fully regaled in the best torn-up jeans money can buy, the finest hairdos done up all disheveled just right, and well-practiced glares of rebellion and general disgust practiced carefully in front of the mirror that afternoon. (Altogether differing from the square adults in style only.)

There they all are: statuesque girls gliding faultlessly, ever so carefully overly made-up, followed by groups of lightly mustached boys, oversize key rings a-jangling at their sides—each group pretending to pay no mind to the other but really wishing for some smooth, affable conversation and frustrated because nobody knows how to do that yet. Younger kids, maybe eighth grade, being squirrelly (just like they are at school) and racing between the parklike benches and concessions that sell candles in the shapes of ice-cream sundaes and Elvis Presley. Older kids, seniors maybe, couples, with their arms wrapped all octopuslike around one another, kind of tottering because it's hard, after all, to walk straight when someone's tugging like that at your waist and shoulder at the same time and your cigarettes are falling out of your pocket and you're trying to get them back in your pocket without having to disengage from your date with whom you have so carefully maneuvered into this entanglement of arms, which says we are a number, we are a date, a couple, and all you guys hangin' around in your guy groups and all you girls hangin' around in your girl groups don't know how to communicate to get something like a relationship started, but we have, and by God, we're hangin' on for dear life.

Into the midst of all this horny, frustrated teenage energy walks Mr. Nehring. With Mrs. Nehring. And the mall is, as I said, the kids' turf. For despite all we may say about the school being for the kids, and how the kids must Assume Ownership of the School, which is truly theirs, it is truly not theirs, for we the teachers and adults make the rules by which the kids must abide, and we the adults make them come there and do what we tell them to do, and we the teachers tell them not to litter on the floor but don't assign them jobs maintaining the premises (which is part of what ownership is all about) because there are laws against forcing kids to do stuff like that, and we the adults pretty much control their lives the whole time they're at school. So when they get to the mall and are quick to realize that the rules in the hallways there are much looser than the rules for the hallways at school, and the stuff you get to do in those rooms off the hallways is much more fun than the stuff you have to do in those rooms off the hallways at school, and having tested the water for freedom to smoke and say, "Fuck you, man," and having found that nobody pays them no mind when they do it, they all come to the same very logical conclusion that the mall is pretty okay. That the mall is for them. That the mall is the place to be, "What it is."

Being off his turf, I daresay, behind enemy lines, stripped of his teacherly authority to enforce school rules, Mr. Nehring becomes just another dude, just another guy in the mall. And as much as Mr. Nehring might like to think he is a pretty hip young teacher at school, he is, after all, just another one of those square adults dodging kids at the mall. But there is one crucial difference between Mr. Nehring and all those other square adults. Mr. Nehring is by day a teacher, so that if perchance Mr. Nehring and a student from school should meet at the mall, the true nature of their relationship will be made plain.

Mr. Nehring and kid in class who is doing well:

"Hey, Mr. Nehring, how's it goin'?"

"Hey, Adam, pretty good. How 'bout you?"

"Can't complain."

And as Mr. Nehring and Mrs. Nehring walk by, they don't look back but they know a whole lot of pairs of eyes are checking them out with a kind of affectionate curiosity. Do you think that's his wife? Is he married? He's wearing jeans. I didn't think teachers went to the mall.

Mr. Nehring and kid who verbally abused teacher who Mr. Nehring earlier that day had escorted to the vice principal's office and who was thereby on the receiving end of school-rule enforcement: No dialogue here. Just a kind of a cold stare from the kid, and Mr. Nehring not knowing whether to wave hi and risk being given the finger or just look the other way. And having passed by the kid, knowing there's at least one pair of eyes following and two lips saying but not quite saying, "Fuck that asshole and his fucking girlfriend."

Anyway, Mr. Nehring and his wife, Mrs. Nehring, go to dinner and then they catch a movie and it's the late show so there are crowds. And after the movie, since it's one of those Cinema Twelve jobs, and several movies are all letting out at the same time, and they're all very popular movies about sex and violence, everybody pours into the Cinema Twelve lobby, which is the same size as it was when Cinema Twelve was Cinema Six, only now there are more people in it. And everybody has to go down one escalator since Cinema Twelve is all by itself way up on the third floor of this mall. And everybody is trying to go down this one skinny down escalator, must be at least five hundred people, and all the while there's that up escalator over there just rolling along ever upward right next to the down escalator rolling along ever downward, only the down escalator is jam-packed full of people and there are hundreds more people waiting in line and they're all waiting impatiently to go down the all-too-slow and inadequate down escalator and there's *nobody* on the up escalator.

So naturally a couple of kids get the idea that maybe they could exit the theater area faster if instead of waiting for that down escalator they set their minds and bodies to beating the up escalator at its own game. Well, the idea has great promise, including the potential for showmanship, since all those people on the down escalator are just standing there gliding slowly down and being in a perfect position to serve as an admiring audience for this feat of youthful prowess. And after all, they may all be squares but squares were once kids, too, who liked the sort of challenge presented by up escalators, which one might possibly try to go down, and though they have lost the vigor and nerve to try it themselves, they surely would admire a couple of kids who might try.

So down start the two kids, their legs moving like jack-rabbits being chased by some fox and their bodies progressing ever so slowly but determinedly forward (surely this is an enactment of those dreams we all have about trying to run but not getting anywhere. And our legs move but our bodies won't). And everybody on the down escalator looks over and watches and pretty soon somebody says, "Yeah, all right!" and there is scattered applause. And the two kids feel encouraged and they pump those legs harder and they're about halfway down now and more people start to cheer them on and now they're about three quarters of the way down and all those square adults are just admiring the hell out of these two kids.

When there at the bottom of the escalator stands this guy in a cheap three-piece suit, walkie-talkie in hand, with a big badge that reads, MALL SECURITY, and he probably obeyed all the rules when he was in high school. And he is flanked by two goons, also in three-piece suits with walkie-talkies and big badges who probably had been honor guards in high school and kept other kids from running in the halls. And there the three of them stand like some brick wall up against which these two jackrabbits have suddenly run. And so the two jackrabbits stop and their little hearts are beating, and quickly all their progress is reversed and now the chief goon with the walkie-talkie is motioning with his hand for the two kids to go back up and come down the right way.

And the two kids are just looking real disappointed, and obviously the sympathy of the crowd is with the two kids. And somebody starts to boo the chief goon and then somebody says boo hiss, and pretty soon the whole down escalator is going boo hiss, and the goons are ignoring us and the two kids start to look elated as they glide in moral victory back to the top and Mr. Nehring and Mrs. Nehring are going boo hiss right along with all the other squares and Mr. Nehring is feeling pretty happy because *for once*, in the anonymity of the mall, he doesn't have to be that goon at the bottom of the up escalator.

5.

The Dusty Trail

• • •

After my ISS duty I eat lunch in the faculty lounge, which is a good name when you consider other "lounges" that come to mind. There is the cocktail lounge: a dark, cavernous addition to motor lodges on highways bypassed by the interstate long ago. The airport lounge: rows of plastic bucket seats bolted to the floor and burdened with travelers wearied by layovers, missed flights, and jet lag. Then there are lounges at bus stations, highway rest areas, certain Laundromats, cinemas, and even public rest rooms. They all have a few characteristics in common. First, they are places that one would choose *not* to lounge in if one had the choice. Second, they are places which by calling themselves lounges try to be attractive but which by virtue of the first characteristic clearly are not. Third, they are places where you go when you are trying to get away from somebody or something.

As I enter, the wall phone is ringing. Isaiah Koff, math teacher, is about to answer. He asks first in a loud voice, "Anybody wanna not be here?" Bill Pierce and Jerry Rubicon raise their hands.

"If it's a parent, I'm not here," says Joe Grossi, standing at the photocopy machine.

"If it's my wife, I'm not here," says Andy Murdoch, eating lunch at the big table at the end of the room.

"Hello, faculty lounge . . . I'll see if he's here. Who's calling, please?" Isaiah covers the mouthpiece with his left hand. "Mr. Grossi, Mrs. Kravetz would like to speak with you. Shall I say you're not here?"

"Oh, Christ. No, I'll take it." Joe walks to the phone.

"Hello, Mrs. Kravetz, how are you? . . . Fine, thank you. . . . Well, Jason did a very good job on the recent unit test, so I thought you'd like to know. That's why I sent the note home. . . . That's right, an 85. . . . Yes, that's a very good score. . . . Well, it was a pretty hard test, Mrs. Kravetz. . . . You're concerned that his grades are slipping? . . . Uh-huh . . . uh-huh . . . yes. . . . I don't know what Princeton's admissions policies are. . . . No, I don't mean to be snide. . . . Yes, you can. . . . All right, Mrs. Kravetz. . . . Very well. 'Bye now."

Joe hangs up. "Jesus Christ, that lady drives me nuts. I send her a goddamn note—"

"We heard it," Jerry interrupts.

"Good gravy," Joe continues, anyway. "I send her a note saying her kid is doing well, and she calls me up and says she's concerned because he's not doing well enough." Joe pads over to the copy machine, shaking his head. Resumes copying. The machine jams. Joe curses, opens the big doors on the front of the machine, and starts looking, turning knobs, flipping levers.

This faculty lounge is also a workroom filled with different machines that teachers need for making copies of things. Photocopy machine, ditto machine (two), and a thermofax machine that turns a printed page into a transparency. Four years ago there was no copy machine in the room, so a bunch of teachers wrote a letter to the superintendent saying how there ought to be one, since photo-

copies look better than dittos. Well, the superintendent fired
back that the district provides photocopy service at the central office and all teachers need to do is send down the master
with one of those forms and they'll get whatever they need.
This letter was posted in the faculty room where it served
to solidify support behind the ad hoc teacher committee,
which sent off another letter. This letter pointed out that
the teachers were aware of this district-provided service but
that since the turnaround time on masters sent to the central
office was about four days, and since lesson plans are worked
up usually the night before, this system was largely useless.
Now the superintendent was upset. Both sides met. The
superintendent said teachers should be planning further
ahead than the night before, and the teachers said, "So when
was the last time you were in the classroom?" and "You've
lost touch and your system is unrealistic," to which the
superintendent, who was pretty mad at this point, replied,
"Tough luck," and the teachers stomped out.

Next Jerry Rubicon, who is a fairly laid-back sort of
person, and who was chief negotiator for the teachers'
union, waited a few days for everybody to cool off. He
then went down to the central office and made what must
have been some generally persuasive remarks because a
week later, lo and behold, there in the faculty lounge, next
to the ditto machine, was an Acme XZ10, not brand-new
but operable. Teachers commenced operating the XZ10.
Pretty soon everybody was running their copies on it and
exclaiming how good their copies were and wasn't this great
and see what a little solidarity will do. Until the XZ10
broke. The serviceman said it was designed for light to
moderate use and there was certainly no way it could possibly keep up with all those handouts teachers needed, and
why did teachers need so many handouts, anyway?

The ad hoc committee went into action again. The superintendent responded that of course the machine was designed for light use because it was intended only for emergency situations such as those rare occasions when a teacher might prepare a lesson the night before instead of four days in advance. This time neither the committee nor Jerry Rubicon were able to provoke change, and after a while people just started to get used to the XZ10 breaking down all the time. They'd tell their students, "Oh, well, the machine broke down," and then write everything on the board and instead of learning something useful, kids would spend half the period copying.

The next September, the ditto machines were gone. The XZ10 was still there, but no longer could teachers run those purple dittos. And boy, were teachers angry. This time the superintendent told the committee that since teachers now had state-of-the-art equipment (to be used, of course, only in emergency situations), they no longer needed those old smelly ditto machines, so over the summer he had the custodians throw them out. Jerry Rubicon was not laid-back about that. The next week, two new ditto machines appeared beside the broken-down XZ10, thus culminating a fitful episode of what we in education must settle for as progress.

There are three tables in the faculty lounge. I steer for the middle one where Jerry and Bill are sitting.

"Oh, God, yes," Bill is saying to Jerry. "Knowledge and ability tests. We're supposed to give them every year now to tenth-graders all across our great state so that superintendents can show off scores and prove how wonderful their programs are."

"I see," says Jerry.

"This sounds like the beginning of a good story," I say, sitting down.

"Yes, indeed. We're talking about the KAT tests—they

can't even spell the goddamn word right," says Bill. "Anyway, they just started them last year. The original intent was to provide a yardstick by which the state could measure the success of English programs, but of course, as always happens with these things, some administrator somewhere put them up on an overhead projector for the board of education. They applauded, renewed the guy's contract, and now overhead projectors around the state are working overtime.

"You know, there's more. This thing is really a classic." Bill's worked up. "On the test there's an objective part and a written part. Now, when we all sat down to correct the essays—I mean the English Department at Amesley—we took it pretty seriously. We gave out very few perfect scores and a lot of kids failed. Well, the next thing we know, the State Education Department has collected all the results from around the state and it turns out that writing ability at Amesley stands well below the state average. Now, are we to believe that kids in a wealthy suburban school district perform that poorly?

"And there's more. Now this is really funny. Turns out teachers in some districts were in possession of the test, with the answer key—it's supposed to be a secure test—two weeks before it was administered. Well, one part of the test is on subject-verb agreement and you have to choose the correct sentence and the choices are something like, 'None of us is going' and 'None of us are going.' Well, someone did an item analysis and found that at most schools, about seventy-five percent of the kids got that one wrong. Come to find out that at Chester, the kids are regular geniuses at subject-verb agreement. Ninety-five percent of the kids at Chester got that one right. Guess who had the test two weeks in advance, guys?"

"Amazing." Jerry bites into his sandwich.

"Incredible." I bite into my sandwich. I like Bill. He's a fighter. In addition to teaching English, he advises the school literary-arts magazine. He and the kids work hard at this magazine; they turn out a good product and have won several awards over the years. Ralph Peters insists every year on reviewing the final pasteups before they're sent to the printer. Pierce, naturally, hates that but must oblige Peters since he is, after all, the principal and "responsible for whatever goes on in this building" (Peters's words). To which Bill Pierce always replies that it's the kids' publication, so we, the adults, should let them take the credit and the responsibility for their work. If the thing wins awards, great. If by its choice of words or commentary it offends a member of the community, then let that person approach the kids, and let the kids deal with the consequences of their own actions (a concept apparently okay to print on walls but not okay to carry into practice). At this point in the dialogue Peters usually runs out of logic and resorts, as persons in power ultimately do when they run out of logic, to the mandate of his office. It's my building. I'm responsible. Period.

Which is all an interesting comment on the nature of authority in public education. Having come into existence during the Industrial Revolution, public education has suffered from an ill-begotten analogy with industry, where authority proceeds from the top down: board, hired officers, middle-level managers, assembly-line workers. Students, of course, don't figure in at all since they, by analogy, are the shapable, inanimate objects of all this machine-age hustle-bustle, the receivers of the action, the ultimate focus of all this industrial might: the product. Raw material become manufactured good.

The history of all the assembly-line workers, whether in the steel industry or the education industry, runs parallel in that we workers, most of whom really do not prefer to be told how to do our jobs (except, of course, certain dead-beats at Chester High School), have struggled for some say in the workplace. Thus Bill Pierce bucks Ralph Peters. Thus teachers fight for their XZ10. Thus the union fights for a contract. Thus the unfortunate but enduring analogy plays itself out to the detriment of all those young people waiting in line to be assembled at the education factory. And, after all, it's with them that the analogy really breaks down. Kids are not rocks.

Jerry, Bill, and Jim all eat their sandwiches. In the back-ground, Joe curses fluently at the still-jammed copy ma-chine. Angelina Alexander is running dittos. Lil Gilliam is collating what looks like a test at the big table by the ma-chines. And at the other table is much uproar among four other teachers over a discussion of veterinarians and pet diseases. Angelina finishes running dittos. She drops her copies into a folder, which she sets on the big table, then pulls a lunch sack out of her canvas bag and sits near Lil.

"I am absolutely furious," says Lil to Angelina. Angelina looks up. Lil continues to collate. Her hair is drawn back tightly. Her face is thin, her eyes dart from page to page. Her arms move with quick, nervous jerks, putting together a set of five sheets, then stapling. Bam! And starts over. "This year's seventh-grade class is the most obnoxious group I have ever seen."

Angelina unscrews her thermos. Lil punches the stapler—bam! "I'm teaching a class on long division and all of a sudden Bill Ching starts cracking his knuckles." Bam! "Well, now this is like a signal, see, because lately the boys in this class have been particularly obnoxious by all cracking their knuckles during lecture." Bam! "So Bill starts cracking his knuckles, then some of the other boys start doing it, but of course"—bam!—"I can't see who, 'cause they only do it when I'm facing the board. They don't want me to see. They want to get me, see." Bam! "Well, finally I say, you guys better stop cracking your knuckles because you have a unit test on Friday. And I don't have"—bam!—"to pass that unit test, but you do. So stop horsing around." Bam! "So then they all start makin' faces like what's she talkin' about, and as soon as my back is turned again, they start crackin' their knuckles." Bam!

I shift my attention to the other table. The uproar has died down. Lane Hall, math teacher, is talking.

"You know, I've been meaning to get my room changed for next year."

"Why is that?" asks Sandy Haverstraw.

"Well, because it's a science room with lab tables and I'm trying to teach math and the kids are always playing with the gas jets and turning the water faucets on and off. I swear, one day somebody's gonna leave one of those jets on and the whole school's gonna blow up. Anyway, I spoke first with Mary"—Mary Robertson is the math department head—"and she says go talk to Ralph. Fine, I say. Well, I go and talk with Ralph and Ralph says why don't I see George about getting it taken care of? Okay, so I go to George, and he tells me that the guidance office is in charge of room assignments. Today I went down to guidance, and can you guess what they said?"

"Go see your department head?" says Sandy.

"You got it," says Lane.

Suddenly Jerry Rubicon is talking to me at my own table.

"Why is it that classroom disasters end with eighth grade?" asks Jerry.

"I'm sorry?" I say.

"How come kids stop having catastrophes in class when they're done with eighth grade?"

"I don't know. How come? Do they?"

Jerry has both Bill's and my attention. "Well, last period was not really extraordinary, but I was just struck by the number of personal disasters that the twenty-odd kids in that class suffered in the space of forty-five minutes. I made a list."

"You made a list?" asks Bill. Bill and I look at each other.

"Yeah." Jerry reaches into his pants pocket. "Here we go. First there was Chrissy, who said her sneaker was stuck in Kimberley's chair, to which I said oh, my goodness, how did it get there? And Chrissy replied that Kimberley had tied it there. To which I replied that Kimberley ought then to untie it. So Kimberley set to untying Chrissy's sneaker. Next Alicia comes up to my desk hiccuping dramatically and pleading that she must go at once to a drinking fountain before she dies of hiccups. Off goes Alicia to the drinking fountain, and a minute later she returns jubilant, eager to tell how she got rid of the hiccups by taking big gulps of water and turning her head upside down or something like that. Anyway, the hiccups are now history and she goes back to her seat.

"Next"—Jerry looks at his list—"I'm walking to the back of the room and I see that Gloria is wiping the top of her desk with a paper towel. I say, Gloria, why are you doing that, and she says because Teige spit on my desk. I look at Teige. Teige says, I slobbered, I didn't spit. Suggesting, I guess, that spit implies malice while slobber implies only dereliction—a lesser crime. Well, Gloria fires back that no, Teige did not slobber, he most definitely spit. So I say, well, Teige, whether you slobbered or spit, if you do something gross on Gloria's desk, don't you think you ought to clean it up?"

Bill Pierce erupts with laughter. It's contagious. Now Jerry and I are laughing, too.

"So Teige says yes, and Gloria goes to throw the paper

towel in the garbage. There's more." Jerry consults his list again. "We're up to disaster number four. Martin goes out for a drink of water. He comes back and a moment later is claiming that someone has stolen his notebook, which was right there on his desk and it certainly didn't just walk away and who did it? I don't know, I say, and before I can launch an investigation, disaster number five is tapping me on the shoulder. It's Terry Moravian, and she's holding up a bloodstained thumb for me to look at. She doesn't say anything, so I eventually say to the thumb, oh, my goodness, what happened to you? Terry replies on her thumb's behalf that there's a nail in her locker and this is the fifth time she's cut her thumb on it. So, of course, I say she should go to the nurse and she ought to see a custodian about having that nail removed. Terry leaves, holding thumb aloft. Well, to round off this series of mishaps, Anthony's pen explodes. Now, I have never personally experienced an exploding pen, but there must be something to it because it happens with some frequency to my eighth-graders and the routine usually goes like this. Kid exclaims out of the blue, oh, my god, my pen just exploded! Everybody looks, eager for drama and misfortune. The kid rises. There is blue ink oozing from the side of his mouth. His face and the surface of his desk is spattered. I say, go to the bathroom at once, don't touch anything. The kid races out. There is much exclaiming about oh, how gross, from around the room. And that's it. That's my list."

Bill and I are roaring with laughter. As much at Jerry's tale as at his absolutely deadpan delivery.

Bill says, "This place is a freakin' three-ring circus." Everybody is looking at the three of us, all laughing at Jerry's story.

So many weary travelers.

"Tell me, Bill"—I decide to change the subject—"where

were you this morning at the end of third period when the ISS kids were tearing apart their cell?"

"Oh, shit. Jesus, Jim," Bill is still laughing. "I'm sorry, it was those KAT tests. I had to get back to my room because the kids are supposed to have exactly forty-five minutes." Bill looks at me. "What happened?"

"Well, actually, all hell broke loose."

"Oh, boy," says Bill.

"I got there the usual time," I begin. "You had just left, I guess, and I walk in and Eddie Hastings is standing on the counter at the front of the room."

"This is gonna be good," says Jerry.

"Yeah, Eddie Hastings is standing on the counter and he's monkeying with the clock, I guess trying to rip it off the wall. Same time, Jason Rosenblum is going through the drawers of the supervisor's desk. And all the other kids are doing squirrely things at their desks, and it was just your basic crazy scene."

"So what did you do?" asks Lil Gilliam. I turn and see Lil sitting erect at the big table with a most serious look of perplexity.

I look Lil straight in the eyes. "Nothing."

Lil looks back; the lines of perplexity freeze hard around her face.

"What am I gonna do?" I say. "I mean, if I had run all over the place screaming and yelling, the kids would have loved it." Jerry and Bill nod in agreement. Lil, firm believer in *discipline*, turns away, disgusted. "Well, I didn't exactly do nothing," I add. "I calmly told the kids to take their seats and I got them going on their assignments, and gradually things started to settle down."

"Yeah," says Jerry.

"Until Belinda Ballou slammed some kid against the wall."

"Oh, my God," says Bill, who is obviously feeling responsible for all this havoc.

"George came up and gave 'em each an extra day in the banana box."

"That whole ISS deal is such a goddamn waste of time," says Jerry.

"It's a prison," says Bill.

"But we are teaching youth about responsibility!" I say.

"Horseshit," says Bill.

Recollection, scene one: It was summer on Cape Cod. I was fifteen, not quite old enough to get a job waitering or even washing dishes. My best friend, Alec, was in the same boat. We'd spend whole days concocting outrageous adventures that ultimately would come to nothing because of some silly detail like our mothers saying no, they wouldn't drive us there to do that because that was dangerous and didn't we have any common sense; or no, that cost too much and why don't you go out and earn money. We'd get discouraged and walk down to the beach and kick sand around and look at girls.

It was on one such occasion, having just been told no, again, when Alec said he remembered seeing plans for a build-your-own hang glider in *Popular Life*. We'd both watched hang gliding off the tall bluffs over the ocean at Truro and had both fantasized about how next summer when we were sixteen and could get jobs and make our own money and have our driver's licenses and wouldn't have to depend on unreliable means of transportation, we'd chip in together and buy a hang glider and drive up to Truro and really do it. Next summer. Well, here was a chance to do it this summer. The idea had merit. According to those directions in *Popular Life*, all one needed was about a hundred square feet of plastic drop cloth, available at the hardware store, and ten bamboo poles used for rolling rugs, which any rug store has plenty of just kicking around in the back room and will happily give away to a couple of enterprising youths at work on a backyard project. And then there was Tom, my brother, who was a "mechanically inclined" builder of models and restorer of lawn mowers. He could build it; better still, he could drive us all up to Truro to test it out. Surely he would go for it—what better incentive could an older brother have than to see his younger brother killed while test-flying a homemade hang glider?

So we set to work building a hang glider. Older brother was persuaded to lay off lawn mowers and was put to work cutting and tying bamboo poles while Alec and I set to measuring plastic drop cloth. Tom turned out, as predicted, to be the real engineering genius behind the project as he made certain necessary modifications in the design since the way they had it in that magazine, he told us, it would never fly. Who were we to question the expertise of one who brings dead lawn mowers back to life? Alec and I looked at each other and said something like, sure, whatever you say.

Shortly the day was upon us. The hang glider was assembled. We set off to Truro, site of mighty bluffs rising about a hundred and fifty feet over the crashing surf. There we would fly our kite. Tom convinced Mom to lend us the family wagon for the morning. Mom no doubt felt no harm would come since older brother was in charge. Additionally, I don't think she fully appreciated what we were going to do. Arriving on location, we trudged up the back side of the dune and began to unfold our creation. It was a huge bat kite, eight feet long, with a twelve-foot wingspan. We hefted the beast, flapped the wings a little, and feeling assured that all joints and seams were secure, decided that we were ready. We stepped out to the edge of the bluff. Way down there, the surf was pawing gently at the sandy beach. Let's do it, said Alec. We walked back to the kite, which was hastily lifted over my shoulders and onto my back. Parallel bars were nestled under my arms for support once in flight. How I was chosen to fly it, I do not remember, but I think it had something to do with me being the smallest, and naturally test pilots must be small—both Tom and Alec agreed. Neither do I remember what exactly went through my mind as I took a running start for the edge of the cliff, but I do remember not wanting to wait a moment longer, as I might get distracted with thoughts of body casts, months spent in traction, wheelchairs, and the like. I did not want to lose nerve. Courage was everything. I raced to the edge of the cliff, popped up the nose of the kite. My feet left the ground. I was flying. Suddenly I was falling. *Bam!* Everything was a jumble—sand, sky, surf, ocean. I was tumbling down the lower portion of the bluff having gone into a nosedive after only seconds of flight. I came to a stop. I was sitting upright. Tom and Alec were striding down the face of the bluff. "That was incredible! Awesome!" They were yelling. I was spitting out sand and wiping off my face. Of course, they did not ask if I was okay, but I did not really expect them to, because in our teenage minds none of us really understood the meaning of danger.

Recollection, scene two: It was April of our senior year in high school. We were the class of 1976. Our nation's bicentennial, as we were repeatedly reminded ad nauseum via television, current-events lessons, morning announcements, Army recruitment posters, etc. 1976. A whole one hundred years would pass before there would be another high-school class historically situated in the manner that we were. That was history that we, in our revved-up teenage minds, could appreciate. It was momentous. It required a response. A gift of sorts to our alma mater marking the occasion. A big gift, ad high-school senior prank, but something more than merely a Volkswagen in the lobby or a cow on the second floor. This required something big.

The idea took shape. Stars, stripes. A big '76. A bicentennial flag. To be painted. The parking lot? Graduation platform? Cafeteria wall? Hood of principal's car? Roof of principal's car? Roof of school building! That was it. A huge red, white, and blue Stars and Stripes painted plainly across the face of that highly visible, steeply pitched slate roof, so that all who drove past would marvel at the combination of daring and patriotism of whoever it was, anyway, that had done that. And there would be a kind of honor among us, the perpetrators, a code of silence. Nobody would ever tell who had done it. And that would be part of what everyone would marvel at. And what a great idea it really was!

Alec and I set to work recruiting. Older brother was out of the picture this time. Wrong class, off to college, and, since the mishap with the kite, which Alec and I regarded clearly as a design flaw, his once-unquestioned engineering ability was now seriously in doubt. Shortly there were five of us. And we started in with weekend planning sessions at locations that would be announced only at the last minute to avoid potential spy infiltration. Special, no-spill paint buckets were designed. The issue of whether to paint with a moon or not was debated and re-debated. The possibility of rain was considered. There were discussions over the relative merits of latex versus oil-based paint. Should we spray or use brushes? What time of night? What sort of harnesses so as not to fall off that steeply pitched four-story roof? And then there was the business of checking out the roof itself. Naturally we all had master keys to the school, and on our unassigned time we would venture out to the rooftop of our huge, multi-winged, turreted, gargoyled school building, being careful to avoid patches of tar and loose slates. It was all definitely doable.

But there was a factor here that had not come into play with the bamboo kite. Standing over the broad plane of blue, green, and gray slate on our practice jaunts to the roof, there was time. Time to consider. Letter from the college-admissions officer: Due to your actions, we regret to inform you . . . Then there were the police and bullhorns in the middle of the night—"Come down off that roof!"—and maybe even handcuffs, and what would my mother say? And how much would a new slate roof cost for the entire front of this public high school? Can you still get slate? What if the paint dripped and we made a mess? Was there such a thing as conscience? Would I crack under police interrogation and name names? Did I really want to ruin my summer vacation? Yes, this was, after all, serious. This time it was not just body casts and wheelchairs and hospital visits from sympathetic cheerleaders, and what a great feat of daring and heroism and gee whiz. It was college and police and bullhorns and my mother and lots of money and shame and ignominy and all the rest.

So we chickened out. I was the first to go, sharing with my buddies most of the aforementioned vision (leaving out only the part about my mother), and then someone else backed out, citing similar concerns. And pretty soon everybody was out. And, amazingly, nobody blamed anybody else. We all wanted to get on with our lives.

But damn, that flag would have looked great.

"Oh, God, please, not in the middle of my lunch." It's Jerry. A bell is ringing. Teachers around the faculty lounge are rising from their seats. They are looking annoyed. I am getting up out of my chair. We are all heading for the door. A bell is ringing. It is a fire drill. Or maybe a false alarm. Or maybe a real, honest-to-goodness fire!

Outside the faculty lounge, the hallway is packed as everybody in the building heads "to the nearest exit." No one seems especially rushed, but the entire mob is moving in the same direction. Which I guess means that the idea of the fire drill, as annoying as it is, works since everybody, at the bell, moves efficiently, without panic, to the doors. It is perhaps one of the few phenomena of public education that might be accurately described as "efficient."

At least from the point of view of crowd control. Seen from an educational point of view, the analysis is a little more complex. Two boys, just ahead of me in the hall, are talking. One is holding up a small piece of white paper with little letters written on it.

"A-B-A-B-C-D-C. It's all I could get, but I think there's a pattern."

The other boy answers, "Okay, so next comes *D*, but then what?"

"It repeats. A-B-A-B-C-D-C-D."

"You really think she's that dumb?"

"I don't know. Maybe she's trying to psych us out. You know, give 'em a test where all the answers follow the same pattern so that only the kids that really know will stick with the right answers."

"I'm not so sure. Are you positive about the first seven?"

"Absolutely. I checked Jason's answer sheet."

I look back a good twenty feet into the crowd and there among the bobbing heads is Mary North, biology teacher, talking with chemistry teacher Tony Desista. Mary is making big I-give-up gestures with her arms. Her test, I guess.

Ahead, two girls stand at a locker. One is working the combination lock.

"Girls, would you please head for the exit?"

"Yeah, just a minute."

"No. Not just a minute. Now, please."

"We're just puttin' our books away." She opens the locker.

"Yeah, well in the time you open your locker the building could burn down around us."

"I don't see any fire."

"That's not the point. Look—"

Slam. The girl shuts her locker door, having deposited her books. She and her friend start walking out with everyone else. I walk with them. "Look," I say, "if you stop at your locker, then other people will see you and say, hey, maybe I should stop at my locker. Pretty soon everybody's stopping at his locker and no one's leaving the building."

"So what? Maybe they shouldn't have these dumb fire drills. I mean, everyone knows there's really no fire. They just gotta meet state regulations so they get their money."

"How do you know it's not a fire?"

" 'Cause it's dumb. We always have these stupid drills. It's like the boy who cried wolf. We have these drills and there's never a fire."

"That's why you stop at your locker?"

"You got it, dude."

We're at the exit. One girl walks through and holds the door for me. I hold it for the next girl. She smiles. We walk out to a beautiful spring day.

I remember a passage from a novel. I don't remember the novel. There is a battle raging and a lone infantryman is creeping through a woodland. In the distance are gunshots and artillery fire. Close by, a bird lets out a momentary song. With this song, the infantryman transcends his embattled circumstances. He is reminded that war is temporary, artificial. But nature, expressed in this bird song, endures. Struck suddenly with the full, bright force of this April day, I feel transcendent. I pad out with everyone else toward the Amesley High football field. The grass is wet. The soil underneath is muddy. I think about the nature of experience within this school building. The idea itself sounds ludicrous. The nature of experience? At Amesley Junior-Senior High School? I can see my kids laughing at the idea. What do we really experience at Amesley? The question is rhetorical. We endure. It is all an extreme contrivance. The very structure of time, regulated to the second by bells, is fitful and episodic. We stutter, helplessly, to the end of the day and eventually, unemphatically, the last bell rings, the artifice relents, and we variously get in cars, climb aboard buses, light up cigarettes, throw books in lockers, shove lesson-plan books in desk drawers, and go home. There has got to be a better way.

6.

What is Research?

• • •

The alarm rings again, signaling the drill is over and we should all return to wherever we left off in our lecture, lunch, test taking (this with renewed confidence), hall roaming, frog dissecting, math equating, and the rest. I slop across the muddy, grassy field, made muddier by a massive trampling. I look at my watch: 11:53. In Amesley time that's almost the end of first lunch. Four minutes to English Eleven. Not enough time to return to the faculty lounge for that half cup of coffee with a little bit of sugar. But it's lukewarm by now, anyway. Somebody will see it and dump it for me. I climb the stairs to Room 25.

I'm early. The room is still. I sit at my desk. Pretty soon everything will be in its usual state of uproar, with kids sliding chairs around, talking, laughing, screaming. With twenty-odd teenagers there's usually a reason for someone to enter the room screaming about some outrage of the moment. Jerry is wrong, after all; regularly occurring disasters do not end with the eighth grade. But for the moment the room is quiet and motionless. I feel a little sentimental. I really like this room. It's a kind of home. To spite its sterile four walls, cold masonry floor, and overhead banks of fluorescent lights, at least one of which is always flickering in death agony, I have filled it over the years with quite a collection of educational junk. There are posters. One that I picked up at a conference on Third World issues shows an enraged African manacled about the wrists. The poster reads, "Break the Links to Apartheid." Next to this is a long row of presidential posters, George Washington at the head of the line. They stretch all the way across the wall and around the corner. There are a few gaps where various presidents have fallen from their places over the years and been mistakenly swept up by zealous custodians. On another wall is a varied collection of student work, a big white oaktag poster with all the countries of Central America, each in a different color. Costa Rica is red, Honduras blue, Belize green, and so on. Another piece of oaktag bears a collage entitled, "Issues of the Third World." An emaciated African child holds out an empty bowl, a cornfield gives way to the encroaching desert, a big Coca-Cola billboard with Arabic writing, a mosque, a church, a modern city, a Masai tribesman. Other student posters crowd the wall.

Then there are bookshelves, at least one against each wall. They are jammed with classroom sets of anthologies, textbooks, handbooks, novels, and workbooks, either purchased by me or inherited from my predecessor. There are magazines: stacks of *National Geographic*, many of them ravaged by makers of collages; stacks of *Newsweek* and *U.S. News and World Report* piled in roughly chronological order. Old issues of *The New Yorker* take up another shelf, the wall above which is filled with *New Yorker* cartoons (the only thing interesting about that magazine, anyway, Mr. Nehring, except maybe the poems, since they're short, but they're mostly dumb). On one wall is the only genuine bulletin board in the room. I'm always getting chewed out by custodians for putting tape on the walls and hammering in tacks and nails, but one bulletin board is simply not enough. At any rate, my one bulletin board serves as current-events space. Although it is indeed current, with clippings and photos from around the world, it also never gets cleaned up, which means that beneath this week's current events are last week's current events and so on, back a good seven years to the time I started at Amesley. I got on an organizing kick one day last September and started pulling down articles, but I started getting distracted by old news, and pretty soon I decided I really didn't want to take down all those articles because they were too interesting, and maybe I could make up a kind of research project for the kids someday with a jazzy title like "Archival Research with Newspapers." But I guess *archive* is a little too formal for my somewhat loosely organized bulletin board. Maybe archaeology, geological layers, something along those lines. Anyway, my organizing kick quickly dissipated and all that news, which is probably a tremendous fire hazard, is still hanging on the wall.

The bell rings. Nothing changes in the room (yet), but all the nice quiet reflectiveness of the moment disappears. Now I've got to start thinking, preparing. I walk to the chalkboard at the front of the room and write, "What is research?" in big letters. English Eleven is currently midway through a unit in which students must ultimately produce a research report, and it therefore seems high time we stopped and considered what it really is we're all doing.

It seems that no matter how I introduce this unit each year, no matter how I try to disguise the fact that students will be *doing research* and will turn in a *term paper*, they always figure it out within the first five minutes. So what you really mean, Mr. Nehring, is we're gonna do a research paper, right? Right. As soon as they figure out what's going on, they collectively begin to work through a kind of grieving process. First, disbelief. You can't do that, we already did one this year in science. Can we still pass if like we just do everything but the term paper? Second, resignation. Well, I guess this blows away spring break. Third, acceptance. How long? Do we gotta have footnotes? Bibliography? We gotta turn in notes? You gonna give us those index cards? How many sources? Can we use the encyclopedia? How many pages? Skip lines?

This need not be a painful experience, I always say, trying to console them. But they always disagree. I tell them I'll help and that they'll all do a great job. Forget it, they always say. They are committed cynics.

Not long ago, Alison Woodward (English department chairperson) and the Admiral called a joint English and Social Studies department meeting. According to the memo that came around there was "deep concern about research papers." This promised to be some powwow, what with two whole departments and "deep concern." The appointed day arrived and we convened in Bill Pierce's room (central location). The Admiral was sitting inconspicuously by the windows when I arrived. I sat down next to him, and in marched Alison. Boom! She dropped a load of texts on the teacher's desk. I looked at the Admiral, who looked back at me and shrugged as if to say, "Don't ask me." It was clear whose meeting this was.

"Could we place the desks in a circle," says Alison. With that, twenty-three teachers start dragging chairs and desks this way and that, just like the kids who we always yell at for dragging and not lifting. Eventually the circle is formed, we sit down, there is whispering, nose blowing, throat clearing, then Alison looks up for silence.

"This meeting is long overdue. First let me give you some background. About ten years ago a committee was established to examine our school-wide policy regarding research papers. Charles, I think you were on that committee, and

Bill, and yes, Grace, and several others. At any rate, the committee set up guidelines to which all teachers were expected to adhere when assigning term papers. The guidelines set forth were what we at Amesley would accept as correct form regarding title page, footnotes, bibliography, and the like. Well, our in-house style sheet, as it were, has languished for about the past nine and a half of those ten years, as everyone has gone willy-nilly back to doing their own thing, and the style sheet has been all but forgotten."

"So let's print off new copies of the style sheet so everybody knows what's expected and be done with it," says Grace.

"I'm afraid it's not that simple, Grace," says Alison.

"I would like to know what our policy is for footnoting," says Charles.

"I tell my students," says Madeline, English teacher, "to insert a superscript number right in the text and then give the citation either at the bottom of the page or at the end of the paper. I'm not a real stickler for detail, I tell the kids, and whether it's on the same page or at the end of the paper, it really doesn't matter."

To this, heads nod in agreement. Then Charles speaks up. "You see, that's where I think we go wrong. I think we need to be consistent"—Hear, hear, says Alison—"about policies just like that so our kids don't become confused. I mean, my goodness, if one teacher says you should place the footnotes at the bottom of the page and then another says no, they belong all together at the end of the paper, and then another teacher says, well, it really doesn't matter, of course kids will be confused. I mean, what kind of a message does that send? That we as teachers don't know what we're doing? It's no wonder kids get so frustrated with term papers."

"Actually, in the journals I read, the footnoting procedure

avoids the whole business of superscript numbers." This is Andy Rourke, and no doubt the fact that he "reads journals" in itself impresses the group. "Most journals seem to follow the procedures of the American Psychological Association these days, which . . . well, it's easier if I show you on the board." Andy goes to the board. "Ahm, let's suppose you're quoting Chaucer, General Prologue, it's like this." Andy writes on the board and explains.

"Well, hold on just a moment, Andy," Grace Haber says, interrupting. "That's an incomplete citation. We're missing publisher, publication date, author's complete name . . ."

"I realize that, Grace," says Andy confidently, having anticipated the question and now answering it. Andy finishes. The group is silent. The group is clearly impressed. Finally Ethel pipes up.

"Well, I just want to say that I think this is a very good idea and that we should all agree here and now to adopt the form of the American Psychological Association as the correct form for citation of sources in all research work conducted by students at Amesley. I think the sooner we impose uniformity in whatever aspect of education that we can, the sooner we begin to cure the ills of today's children. No, really. I think that kids today are so . . . so disorganized and out of sorts primarily because there is no order enforced from above. I mean, look at our school. Kids roaming the halls, smoking in the bathrooms until they're blue in the face, not doing homework, wearing rags and calling it fashion, playing their Walkmans, listening to their rock and roll. It is truly disgraceful. It is truly disgraceful! Alison, I move that we adopt this footnoting procedure as the official method of citation for Amesley Junior-Senior High School."

"Well, wait a minute." Grace interrupts again. "I hear what you're saying, Ethel, and I agree with you, too, but

I just think we need to look at this a little before we go ahead. For instance—and, Andy, this is a question, I guess, for you—let's suppose you have a work without an author; I mean, something like an almanac or a general encyclopedia. This method of footnoting will not, at least as far as I can see, accommodate that kind of citation."

Thus proceeded the multidepartmental footnote pow-wow toward a not-very-swift conclusion, ending with a decision to retain traditional footnote procedure until such time as a committee could be convened (a footnote committee?) to examine alternatives.

You ask why my students are committed cynics?

English Eleven begins to file into the room. I move to the side of the room, rest my arm on the top of the filing cabinet, and think through the lesson as the class assembles. Pretty soon they're all in their seats, all too ready to go wherever I choose to lead. Walter Tracy, Julie Kosinski, Karen Moramarco, Karen Frisby, Andy Moreno, Robert Malter, and Kathy Friedman. Then there are the four Michaels: Michael Theer, Michael Heber, Michael Bradington, and Michael Ronald. The last Michael I'm always confusing with Ronald Rechter, who sits one row up and across. To make matters worse, Michael Theer and Michael Heber like to be called Mike, whereas Michael Bradington and Michael Ronald prefer Michael. Ronald Rechter prefers Ronald, which means Mr. Nehring sometimes gets very confused. If Mr. Nehring stands at the right front corner of the room, all the Michaels line up diagonally and sometimes when called on to answer a question will get as confused as Mr. Nehring. Which one of us do you want, Mr. Nehring? Michael, I insist, pointing clearly at Michael. This only deepens everyone's consternation.

The group, twenty in all, is subdued today. There is less than the usual noise that accompanies a class full of sixteen-

and seventeen-year-olds. From my post at the filing cabinet I call to Alice Shuchman in the back row in a voice loud enough to get everyone's attention. "Alice Shuchman, would you please read, in a nice loud teacherly voice, the question that appears on the chalkboard at the front of the room? And please wait until you have everyone's attention."

Alice waits, then reads, "What is research?"

"Alice"—I shake my head—"I know you have more heart than that. Now look, I want you to imagine you've just spent six hours in the library. Your eyes are bleary and watering from the microfilm machine where you've been meticulously reviewing every page of *The New York Times* from January to June of 1928. To your great dismay, you have not found what you were looking for. Your entire hypothesis seems to be ill founded. You're no longer certain of what it really is that you are looking for. You're confused. You're tired. You begin to question the meaning of life and you cry out with every ounce of energy left in your broken frame, 'What *is* research?' Now cry it out, Alice, with all the desperation you feel inside you."

"What *is* research, Mr. Nehring?"

"Beautiful, Alice. Beautiful. Now, who can answer Alice's desperate plea?"

"I have no idea. I'd like to know myself," says Andy Moreno.

"Andy," I say, "by the end of this period, I guarantee you will know the answer to this question. Is there an answer to Alice's question?" I ask the class. "I mean, we've been doing this unit on research for the last few weeks, and all of you are supposedly engaged in a research project. So you must all have some sense of what research is, right?"

"It's when you go to the library," says Robert.

"Well, that's a start," I say. "Let's see now, going to the library. If I'm living out on the street and I need a place to go get warm and I walk into the library, am I doing research?"

"I mean, like using the card catalog and stuff," says Robert.

"Oh, okay. What's the difference?"

Jane Alden speaks up. "The difference is that the person at the card catalog is looking for something."

"Hmmm," I say. "I suppose the poor guy from the street is looking for something too."

"Yeah," says Frank Resnick. "He's looking for a place to get warm."

"So are they both doing research?" I ask the class.

"Maybe," says Robert.

"Maybe, but not really," I say. "Let's try a new tack. Is there any way to conduct research besides going to the library?"

Loretta DiPolito speaks. "With my paper that I'm doing on Vietnam, I'm interviewing some veterans from the war."

"Is that research?" I ask the class.

"Yes," they chorus back.

"So, then, what do going to the library and interviewing veterans have in common?"

"In both cases you're looking for something," says Karen Moramarco.

"But I thought we said the poor guy from the street was looking for something too."

"But it's not the same," Karen insists.

"I agree, Karen," I say. "It's not the same. But what's the difference?"

"The difference is that the bum is looking to get warm and the people doing research are looking for answers."

"Yes," I say. "They're looking for answers. And if you are looking for an answer, it means you must have been asking some questions. So what is research?"

"Looking for answers?" says Karen.

"Sure. Why not?" I say. "Whether you're a little kid in third grade trying to find out where all the little birdies go in winter, or whether you're some nuclear physicist trying to figure out how to control a fission reaction, it's the same basic thing that you're trying to do. You're trying in some systematic way to answer a meaningful question or series of questions. That's what research is. You all are conducting research right now. You are trying to answer in some systematic way the questions that you laid out in your research proposals last week. After you've found the answers, then you're going to have to write it all up in a report—that's what's due next week. Now look, your report is really very simple. All you need to say, essentially, is here are the questions I set out to answer, here are the answers I found, and here's how I found them."

"What about footnotes?" asks Robert.

"Listen, don't get uptight about footnotes. In fact, forget you ever heard the word. Let's suppose all twenty-one of us are sitting around one day with nothing to do. Then suddenly Robert says, 'Hey, I got an idea. Let's have a party.' So we have a party and it's a big success, and then Julie says, 'So wasn't that a great idea I had about having a party?' Well, Robert and his buddies will say, 'Whaddaya mean, your idea, it was Robert's idea,' and then everybody gets upset. But then somebody in the group says something like, 'Credit where credit is due,' and, after all, it was Robert's idea, and then everyone says okay and nobody's upset anymore. Now when you do research and you mention some idea that somebody else came up with, you've got to give that person credit for his or her idea. It's only fair. That's what footnotes—I'm sorry I said the 'f' word—are really all about. That's all.

"Now, Robert, to answer your question, if you want to

put those little 'f' notes at the bottom of the page or at the end, fine. If you want to put the author's name in parentheses in the text and then give a full citation at the end of the paper, joy go with you. I really don't care how you do it. But I do care that you *do* it. I care that you give credit where credit is due."

Teachers have grown weary of telling kids why they gotta do stuff. Worse yet, I fear we've stopped asking *ourselves*. So we tell the kids with knuckleheaded determination that they gotta do it, so just do it. And when pressed, we say it's on the test or it's just something that an educated person should know. So a kid tries his best, under the circumstances, to learn what he must conclude is meaningless, and he either learns it or doesn't learn it or he learns it partially, then turns around and forgets it completely because after all it's meaningless. The next year, when a different teacher starts teaching the same stuff, the kid figures, why ask why we gotta do it since we gotta do it, anyway. Third time around, if the kid's sense of justice has not been completely subdued, acceptance turns to resentment: All right, I'll do it, dammit. While all this is going on in the kid's mind, the teachers follow a related mental path. You learned this last year, says the teacher. Don't you guys remember anything? Then, in the faculty room, teachers talk. We teach this every year to these kids, and you'd think by the time they reach high school, they'd know it. If concern among the staff becomes great enough, then a departmental meeting is called (sometimes multidepartmental) and at this meeting all jointly exclaim how terrible it is that kids don't know this stuff, and it's TV, and it wasn't this way twenty years ago, and it's time we set up some rules and policies. If there are educationists in the group, they talk about "articulating the curriculum," which means that instead of making the kids do the same meaningless stuff every year, we make them do a little of it each year on the incorrect assumption that the kids can't do it because it's too difficult, when of course the real reason is that they don't do it because it's meaningless.

Jeff Danzig was a student in my class of non-heterogeneously grouped "dumb kids" (that's what everyone thought but no one said). Jeff had basic skill deficiencies (no doubt because the curriculum had not been articulated). He couldn't use the textbook index or the table of contents or the glossary. Neither could he find the main ideas in reading selections in those workbooks, nor identify the action words. One day the kids were doing some sort of reading assignment and I was making the rounds helping individuals locate main ideas and generally attempting to address all those basic skill deficiencies. I came to Jeff. Jeff was not doing his assignment. Instead he was reading *Buy Direct From U.S. Government and Save.*

"What are you doing, Jeff?"

"I'm lookin' for spare parts."

"Spare parts for what?"

"My Jeep."

"Huh. That's pretty interesting. How does this book work?"

"Well, it's pretty easy, really. You see, you got all this government-surplus stuff at the beginning. And they tell you cars, trucks, radios, airplanes, and they got the page where it's at, see. Now, like, I need new fenders for my Jeep 'cause they're all rusted out. So here it lists Jeeps, and they got all the years and my Jeep's a 1978. So I look at page 265. Now, on page 265, see, they got this picture of a Jeep, like a diagram, and all the parts have numbers and you just write down the number of the part you want, and then you go down the price list that they send with the book and then fill out the order form at the back and send it in."

"And you've used this book to order parts?"

"Oh, yeah. A few weeks ago I got a surplus carburetor."

"Hmm. That's pretty good, Jeff. Have you done your assignment?"

"What was it?"

"Never mind, Jeff. Order your fenders."

Around the room, my English Eleven students are getting fidgety. I guess that not everyone shares Robert's concern over footnotes. It is time to move on. A few years ago some of my students came to me after class and said, "Mr. Nehring, we don't know what you want exactly for these research reports." So I tried to explain it to them but it just wasn't making any sense. And one of them finally said, "You know, what would really help is if you gave us a model research paper that we could read so we'd know how to write ours." Everybody agreed. So next year Mr. Nehring sat down and wrote a sample research paper and I've been giving it out to students ever since.

"You gonna give us them sample term papers you talked about?" asks Tony Stefan on cue from the back row.

"Absolutely. Matter of fact, Tony, I'm going to give you one right now."

I walk to the head of each row and hand four copies of my model term paper to the kids sitting there. They pass them back. Soon everyone has a copy of "The High Cost of Movie Tickets" by Gloria Schnerd. Along with Gloria's paper, each student receives a list of guide questions, which if they answer thoroughly and in order will yield one perfect term paper organized much like Gloria's. Together we will review the guide questions, then read the model research report and see how Gloria Schnerd answers all the guide questions in the report. Each year for the past few years I've done this activity with my English Eleven classes, and each year it has met with universal acclaim. In fact, by the time we get to this point in the research unit, most kids are beginning to break free of their term-paper phobia. Some even achieve a kind of transcendent consciousness in which they actually enjoy conducting research. I do not attribute this achievement to marvelous teaching, but I do believe it has something to do with two important assumptions. First, that kids need to know why they gotta do the stuff; and second, that they need to be shown how to do it.

Sarge Engstrom believed it was very important that students be exposed to research during their high-school years. And to achieve this laudable goal, Sarge regularly assigned a term paper to his freshman classes in the spring of the year. He allowed his students to pick their own topics, a practice to which Sarge seemed embarrassed to admit, as though it were some weak-kneed concession to liberal-mindedness. Then came the requirements: double-spaced, typed, one-and-a-quarter-inch margins all the way around, five sources listed in correct bibliographic format, and minimum length of ten pages. All papers not meeting these exacting standards would be returned with no credit. Troops, fall out!

I could always tell when Sarge's kids were into their term papers. The tone of the freshman hall between classes went from frantic to neurotic. Additionally, signs of the students' displeasure with Mr. Engstrom's assignment appeared. "Engstrom sucks" showed up with greater than usual frequency on book covers, lavatory stalls, and desktops. Engstrom referred to these annual symptoms as the normal signs of "creative tension." He also called it "Sturm and Drang."

The Sturming and the Dranging carried on for exactly two weeks, from assignment date to due date. It would intensify near the end—all the windows in Sarge's classroom were broken one year on the night before the due date—then would suddenly, quietly, dissolve. Of course, this was supposed to be independent research, which meant that Sarge, on principle, refused to answer questions or assist students in locating information. "Kids need to learn to be self-sufficient," Sarge said.

Next came the correcting. Sarge experienced a kind of Sturm and Drang himself as he plowed through a hundred and thirty ten-page essays, typed, and mostly copied from encyclopedias. Sarge's big concern was plagiarism, about which he complained bitterly and often. He was fond of exposing students in front of their classmates, and his favorite story included such a scene.

"Smith, stand and read your report to the class, starting with the first paragraph."

"Yes, sir." Brian Smith starts to read. "The Alhali people of the western sahel inhabit an arid land from which these resourceful nomads eke out a simple, pastoral existence . . ."

At this point Sarge begins reading from the *Atlas of the World's People*. Engstrom and Smith read together. "Warm African days are spent tending small herds of goats and sheep, which to the Alhali serve as food supply, money, and symbol of prestige."

Brian stops reading. Sarge stops reading. Brian looks at Sarge. Brian looks at his classmates. "Well, that doesn't prove nothin'," Brian finally says.

"Son, it's adequate proof to me that your work has been plagiarized. That is to say, it is not your work at all. It is the work of others. And it is very good work for which others deserve an A+ and you deserve a zero. Be seated."

In the year before Sarge retired, plagiarism took a leap

into the twenty-first century at the deft hands of Matthew
Jordan, Amesley's most promising computer whiz kid.
Faced with the task of filling ten pages with text and having
no idea how he could fill those ten pages with the product
of his own research, whatever that is, Matthew logically
concluded, along with many of his classmates, that since
there was already a whole world filled with books, and since
many of those books were just filled with stuff about African
tribes and deserts and jungles and all those things that Mr.
Engstrom was always talking about, one could just use the
material that was readily at hand. Only Matthew, recog-
nizing that the assignment was just a meaningless school
task, anyway, was annoyed that he would still have to type,
double-spaced, one-and-a-quarter-inch margins, all of those
ten pages. There must be a better way.

Enter the personal computer, outfitted with word-
processing software and modem linking the user to a world
of pre-processed information located in commercial data
bases around the nation. Matthew set to work. Actually it
wasn't much work at all, which for Matthew was the beauty
of it. It was simple. Matthew dialed the number of a company that provided home-computer users with access to *The
Acme American Encyclopedia.* He punched in a few key words
on his keyboard, and in a few moments up on the screen
appeared an article on the effects of the Aswan Dam on the
ecology of the Nile River Basin. Matthew pressed a few
more keys and the entire article was loaded into the computer's memory. Next, using the word processor, Matthew
began to manipulate the text: moving paragraphs, changing
sentences, deleting text that sounded too adult. Finally he
set the margins—one and a quarter inch exactly—punched
a few more keys, and out of the printer emerged "How the
Aswan Dam Changed Egypt" by Matthew P. Jordan. The
whole assignment took less than a half hour to complete,

including bibliography, adjusted to possess some realistic errors. It was a wonder to behold.

Matthew was duly proud of his accomplishment. And being, in addition to a computer whiz kid, an entrepreneur of sorts, Matthew began offering his services for a fee to Mr. Engstrom's freshman classes. Matthew was doing a thriving consulting business when the roof caved in. It was inevitable that a service in such demand to Mr. Engstrom's students would eventually become known to Mr. Engstrom. Somebody blabbed. Matthew got called to the principal's office, parents were phoned, letters went into files, and Matthew was assigned an unprecedented five days' internal suspension. Four accomplices received lesser terms of two days.

When kids are not taught how to do something, they learn how not to do it. Teachers call this cheating. Kids call it survival.

When I was in first grade, my teacher, Mr. Foote, told me that when someone cheats, he only hurts himself. The reason, of course, would be that by cheating, one deprives oneself of an opportunity for valuable learning. When I was in first grade, I believed this, as did all of my classmates. I think we continued to believe it in second grade, too. In fact, it may have stuck with us all through elementary school, but by the time we got to high school, I think there were very few of us who really believed that we were hurting ourselves by looking at that answer sheet that the kid in the next row had laid all too visibly at the edge of his desk, or by paraphrasing that encyclopedia article on North American Indians in our term paper. Or by rewriting the book jacket to serve as the book report for that 300-plus-page book that nobody really read, anyway. Some of us, of course, refrained from doing those kinds of things, but not because we thought we would "hurt ourselves." Rather we believed it was just wrong to do that kind of thing. Or we were afraid of what our mother would say if she found out. But we had long before stopped believing there was innate value in learning, and that cheating robbed us of something precious. We had come to believe that the grade we got on what we were supposed to have learned *did* have value.

"Mr. Nehring, are you going to give us a grade for our rough draft?" We're back in English Eleven.

"No, Tony. The purpose of turning in the rough draft is to get some feedback on it so that you can make revisions for your final report."

"But that's not fair. Suppose we turn in the rough draft but never finish the report. Does that mean we get a zero?"

"Well, why don't we cross that bridge when and if we come to it." My modest effort to de-emphasize grades is thwarted by my students' years of experience in the system.

A good ten minutes remain in the period.

"Are there any problems that anyone in the class has encountered in his or her research that you'd like to share with the group?"

About eight hands go up. Right question, I guess.

"Michael. No. I mean Michael . . . Michael Theer."

"Well, I'm doing my thing on Agent Orange that was used during the Vietnam war, and I'm trying to find out if it's harmful—I mean, if it causes cancer and stuff."

"Very interesting. Does it cause cancer?" I ask.

"Does it cause stuff?" asks Andy Moreno.

"Well, I don't know if it causes cancer," says Michael. "I read this federal study, see, and they said the worst thing it causes was some minor skin problem. And then I read this other study and they said it causes cancer"—Michael turns to Andy—"and stuff."

"My uncle died of that," says Andy.

"So you've got several different sources, all telling you different answers to your research question, and you're getting frustrated because you don't know what to write, right?"

"Exactly."

"What do you think you should write?"

"I don't know."

"Well, let's suppose that you write this paper and in it you say that Agent Orange has been clearly, indisputably linked with certain kinds of cancer. And then let's suppose that you send your article to the *New England Journal of Medicine*, and lo and behold they publish it. The article comes out in the next issue, you're proud as can be, and the next thing you know, the phone is ringing and it's Joe Blow, Ph.D., head of the government team that said that Agent Orange only causes skin irritation. Why might Joe be upset?"

"Because I didn't say anything about his study."

"Right," I say. "Now, if you said definitively that Agent Orange does not cause cancer, you might get phone calls from the other guys who say it does. So what do you think you should do to avoid getting phone calls?"

"Tell both sides."

"Exactly."

"But that doesn't answer my research question."

"That's right," I say.

"But . . . but . . . is that okay? I mean, will I get points taken off?"

"Michael, believe me when I tell you that if you do not come up with an answer that no other person on this planet has been able to come up with, you will not have points taken off. I mean, look, we've got to deal with points because we're in school, and for better or worse, school is all about points. So, yes, you get a grade on your report, but you are doing some very meaningful research here. You are uncovering some very important ideas, such as the fact that nobody seems to know just what the effects of exposure to Agent Orange really are. This is not about points. It's about cancer and research and major litigation and the credibility of the federal government and the liability of the federal government, and it goes on and on. Okay?"

"Yeah," says Michael.

"Next question." Several hands go up. "Julie."

"Mr. Nehring, I can't find anything on my subject."

"Remind me, Julie, what is your subject?"

"Vietnam veterans."

"Ah, another Vietnam paper. Hmm, let's see. Wait a minute; you can't find *anything* on Vietnam veterans? Have you looked?"

"Yeah." She looks down.

"I'm sorry. I don't mean to be snide. Sometimes what looks easy to an outsider is really very hard once you get into it. Obviously you've looked. Tell me where."

"I've been through every encyclopedia and almanac in the school library, and I think just about every one at the Amesley Public Library."

"Uh-huh, so you've looked at encyclopedias. Have you looked anywhere else?"

"Where else is there to look?"

I try not to sound snide this time. "Why don't we throw the question to the class? Where else can Julie look? Yes, Loretta."

"Well, I'm doing my paper on how shopping malls are becoming more and more popular, and I used something . . . I think they call it Magazine Info. It's really easy. Like all you do is type in your subject—it's all computers—and then you get this printout of all these articles in magazines on your subject."

"Yes, absolutely," I say.

"How about the card catalog?" says Michael Ronald.

"Very good, Ronald. What else?"

"Reader's Guide."

"Vertical file."

"Your mother." Everybody laughs.

"That's not a bad idea, really," I say. "Why isn't that such a bad idea?" The class is baffled. "Well, let's suppose you're doing a research project on public attitudes toward the Vietnam war during the presidential campaign of 1968."

"Oh," says Walter Tracy in the first row. "If she was around in 1968, and she had an attitude about the war, then you could ask her what it was."

"Right," I say. "Is there anybody else in our community who was around during the Vietnam war who might be able to help Julie?"

"What about Vietnam veterans?" Robert Malter asks.

"What about 'em? Why not?" I say.

"Okay," says Julie, "but how do I find 'em and, you know, like get them to talk to me?"

"Good question," I say. "Anybody have a suggestion?"

"My uncle belongs to the American Legion," says Kathy Friedman. "I bet he'd help you out. Maybe he could introduce you to some of the other guys there and set up an interview."

"I don't know," says Julie. "Maybe I should try a different topic."

School is a world unto itself. Kids grow up in this world and acclimate themselves to it. They learn how to get by in it—for better or for worse. They learn that grades matter and, as far as the adults are concerned, nothing much else. If they master the game, they feel safe. Until somebody stirs the waters. You mean, I gotta interview real people? Man! You mean, the answer's not in the encyclopedia? You gotta be kidding! You mean, I gotta go to the public library? Be real!

The bell rings. Students file out. Dale Rea, Candy Donnegan, and Frank Resnick stop at my desk.

"Mr. Nehring," begins Dale. "We feel uncomfortable with the way you want us to do our term papers."

"Oh," I say. "How's that?"

"Well, in other years it seems all our teachers have had us do it a certain way, and now you want us to do it a different way."

"How do all the other teachers have you do it?"

"Well, you know," says Frank, "the usual way, with note cards and then footnotes."

"Yes," says Candy. "And usually the topics are assigned and the teacher makes sure that the library has the right stuff."

"Yes," says Frank, "and that makes it a whole lot more straightforward. I mean, you don't have to go and try to find people to interview, or I know some students in this class, Mr. Nehring, who've been forced to go to the university library because they couldn't find what they needed here. With all respect, Mr. Nehring, I don't think students should have to go out of their way like that."

"And why is that?" I ask as evenly as possible.

"Because this is school, Mr. Nehring," says Frank. "I mean, we're just kids, after all. We're not real researchers. We're supposed to be just *learning* how to do this stuff."

"And when do you become real researchers, Frank?"

"After we're done with school. Or maybe never, if we like go into advertising or something."

"So what we want to know," says Dale, winding up for the pitch, "is if we could just do our term papers the way we're used to instead of the way you're asking us to."

"Absolutely not."

7.

Green Lawns and Good Schools

• • •

Period seven: unassigned time. I have until 1:37 P.M. to run errands, plan lessons, make phone calls, duplicate student materials, read essays, go to the bathroom; in short, everything I need to do in the course of a day but cannot do when I'm teaching a class. As usual, today's unassigned time is already oversubscribed. What with all the unresolved matters that arise in the course of a teacher's day, I could probably fill a good three hours with phone calling alone. The number-one priority, however, is to go to the bank. I fear a bad-check notice is imminent with the mail. Although payday is not until tomorrow, June Henrikson, processor of paychecks in the main office, is usually willing to hand checks over by noon of the day before. The plan is to make a beeline for the main office, pick up check, sign out of building, run down to bank, and make it back in time for period eight. If the line at the bank is not too long, I can just make it. I've done it before.

I lock my door and start down the hall. I pass Skip Klein's

room. Behind Skip's closed door I hear uproarious laughter and Skip's voice in the midst of it.

"I'm sorry, Amy, but you really set yourself up for that."

"That's okay, Mr. Klein."

Across the hall is Roberta James. Her door is open and I see about half of my sixth-period class in Roberta's columns and rows, including two of the four Michaels. The class is silent, orderly, apparently waiting for instructions from their teacher.

Next down the hall is Janet Pauley, who, as I pass, is standing before her class, hands clasped, arms upraised, face suppliant. She says, "Dear students, I cannot take your final exam for you. You will be the ones sitting there in the gym on a hot afternoon in June, and if you do not know your formulas, you will be the ones sitting in a hot classroom in July and August sweating through six weeks of summer school while I am enjoying my cabin on the lake."

Next comes Jerry Rubicon. Jerry's door is open and his class of eighth-graders is in its usual state of creative uproar. Jerry's kids appear to be arranged in groups of four or five, but a few of the kids are in motion, racing between groups and consulting with Mr. Rubicon. I pause a minute and study the kids. Almost without exception, each one bears a look of determination. Each one is engaged. This is a good class. The kids are enthusiastic and involved. On the face of it, though, the class is a mess. Kids are racing every which way, Mr. Rubicon is barking directions with grunts and half-sentences, there is laughter and talk and occasional vulgar language. It is the sort of class that Ralph Peters tries to discourage. In fact, Jerry has told me on several occasions about the unsatisfactory observation reports that Ralph has written on his classes, with multiple references to a lack of order and lack of control, that sort of thing.

I come next to Ethel Port's room. Ethel, standing before the class, reads a familiar poem.

> *"Hold fast to dreams*
> *For if dreams die*
> *Life is a broken-winged bird*
> *That cannot fly.*
>
> *Hold fast to dreams*
> *For when dreams go*
> *Life is a barren field*
> *Frozen with snow."*

"Remember, class, we're trying to figure out how the rhythm of this poem mirrors the poem's sense—whatever that means. Take a close look at the poem. If you were going to set this poem to music, to make it into a song with a regular beat, which two lines would be difficult to fit in?" Ethel reads the poem, exaggerating the stressed syllables. "Which two lines seem to kind of stand out as being longer than the others? Yes, Joe."

I step to the side of Ethel's doorway, just out of view.

" 'Life is a broken-winged bird' and 'life is a barren field.' "

"Exactly, Joe. Now look. In this poem, life is compared to two things. Who can tell me one of the two things life is compared to? Yes, Heather."

"A bird."

"Very good. A bird. A 'broken-winged' bird. What is the other thing that life is compared to in this poem? Janine?"

"It's compared to a barren field."

"Yes, excellent. Now think about that. 'Life is a broken-winged bird' and 'life is a barren field.' Why is it fitting that the rhythm of these two lines in particular breaks away from the rhythm of the rest of the poem?" No one answers. "Do a broken-winged bird and a barren field fit in with the idea of nice dreams about life?" The class choruses a hesitant no.

"Oh, I get it!" a girl blurts out.

"What do you get, Erika?" asks Miss Port.

"Well, the ideas in these two lines, about the bird and the field, don't fit in with the dream. And the rhythm in the two lines doesn't fit in with the rhythm everywhere else in the poem."

"Yes. The rhythm mirrors the sense of the poem," Ethel reiterates.

"Yeah, well, that's like what I said," says Erika.

"That's *just* like what you said, Erika," Ethel affirms. The idea connects for Erika. She possesses the concept and has come to possess it through her own effort. Ethel, showing off some considerable pedagogical skill, has lit the path along the way. A small victory has been won.

My forty-five minutes of free time is slipping past. I step to mid-hall and walk quickly toward the office. On either side, classes are under way. Teachers talking, kids writing, groups discussing, books being read, ideas being shared. Inside each of these classrooms is much purposeful activity. Each teacher, a craftsperson of more or less talent (mostly more), carefully shapes the experience of his or her students into something meaningful and worthy. What an enterprise, really, to direct so minutely the attention of so many people. It is in the individual classroom that the business of public education establishes its worth. There, something of a community struggles for identity, but it is continually disintegrated at the end of every "period." The structure of school is an intrusion on the nascent efforts at learning and teaching that go on in a good class. The classroom is a community within the school, which is a noncommunity. Teachers do what they can behind closed doors for forty-five minutes, then release their students into the wilderness of the school day.

The hallway widens at the student foyer. Amos Morley is slumped against the far wall; his eyes are wide, bright, and blank, and they remind me of a television left running with no one in the room.

Amos sees me. "Hey, dude! You on patrol again?"

"No, Amos. Off duty. Listen, do you ever go to class?"

"I got my four subjects and the rest is free time."

"So you got four periods of free time? You don't get homework?"

"No, man. My teachers don't give no homework."

"You passing all your courses?"

"Oh, yeah, they're easy."

I think about Jerry Rubicon's students—such intensity of expression. I think about Amos Morley and other kids I see around the halls—such aimlessness. Aimlessly Junior-Senior High School, I think. The halls are like some ghetto scene, with all the guys hangin' out on front stoops and street corners, no sense of advantage or opportunity. Public school is like a poorly administered welfare system that seduces creative minds into mindless conformity. The system encourages poverty of mind. Just as in the ghetto, the human spirit sometimes strikes out against its circumstances of enforced degradation. The school experiences its own riots and vandalism—unruly classes, graffiti, broken windows, cherry bombs in the toilet, smoking in the boys' room. Then we school people respond with policelike enforcement, with "crackdowns" and "busts." Police and school officials share a common vocabulary. And at school the larger problem is avoided, as its most apparent symptom—disorder—is continually addressed with fanatic determination. But like the proverbial criminal whose bloodied hands cannot be washed clean, the walls are quickly recovered with graffiti, the bathrooms get hit again, and that last-period class continues to act up.

June Henrikson is at her desk. The checks are in her hand.

"June, any chance a financially strapped employee could obtain his paycheck a few hours ahead of schedule?"

"Yup." June looks through the stack of envelopes. "Here you go." I sign my name, to show I am leaving the building, and head for the parking lot.

The parking lot is a place of high interest. It is much more than merely a place to park cars. Although that very fact has become a big-time issue, due to the presence of too many cars and not enough parking lot. So who gets to park? Well, teachers and administrators first, since they make the rules. Only how does Frank, the parking lot attendant, tell a student car from a teacher car? Simple, reasoned George Handelman, in whose lap the weighty responsibility of parking-lot supervision rests. All the teachers will affix stickers to their bumpers identifying their cars as teacher cars. Thus were stickers printed, complete with gummy backs, and numbers assigned, two per teacher, since some teachers have two cars, and before the assembled faculty, George unveiled his plan one day last year, stickers in hand. Then things started to get complicated. Bernice objected to labeling her car as an Amesley teacher car, claiming (justifiably) that it might become the target of vandalism when parked in places other than school. Tony Desista pointed out that unless those stickers have pretty strong glue, kids will be ripping them off in no time and there will be a thriving black market in teacher car stickers. The sympathy of the faculty seemed to be leaning toward Bernice and Tony, and soon George threw up his arms and said something about "back to the drawing board." At the next meeting George announced a new plan of attack. Instead of affixing stickers to bumpers, each teacher would be issued a plastic tag to be hung from the rearview mirror whenever the car was parked at Amesley. Otherwise it could be removed, and Bernice and everybody else could travel incognito to the mall. This worked.

Only that being able to distinguish the teacher cars from the other cars did not solve all problems. Last spring, the problem started to get pretty bad. "Other" cars started appearing with greater frequency in the teacher lot, and kids arriving late to homeroom complained that they had driven to school and, not finding space to park, had gone back home for a driver who could drop them off. (Why they could not have taken the district-provided school bus was not always clear.) Additionally, cars lined the surrounding streets, illegally, and littered the lawn around the parking lot. Ralph and George decided it was time for a crackdown. An edict was promulgated. All illegally parked cars will be subject to towing. Period. That meant "other" cars parked in the teacher lot and any car parked on the lawn. This worked fine until the assistant superintendent's car was towed. Poor Fred had arrived at the high school for a nine-o'clock meeting and, not finding any available space, had parked on the lawn. The edict was rescinded.

It was then decided that all cars belonging to teachers and students would be required to display the same plastic tags that the teacher cars already had, this being the only aspect of the program that still seemed to have any merit. Since there were not enough spaces for students who wanted them, plastic tags would be distributed to seniors first, then to juniors and to others, on the basis of need. The senior part of this idea was no problem, but the basis-of-need part proved to be prickly. Alice, a junior, has a job that she must start fifteen minutes after school lets out. It takes her ten minutes to drive to the job. Alex, also a junior, must make frequent trips to the orthodontist; his appointments have to be scheduled early so that he may return to Amesley for baseball practice. Eric, a sopho-more, has to pick up his mother from one job and drive her to another before continuing on to his own job, which begins exactly one half hour after school ends. Who gets the plastic tag?

This system, currently in force, seems to have provided a temporary, however flawed, stay against total chaos. George Handelman, giver of plastic tags, is simultaneously villain and hero among kids who vie for parking rights. But the system does not address the persistent problem of finding space for visitors whose cars are indistinguish-able from the illegally parked student cars that no doubt occupy the visitor spaces from time to time. The only real solution, according to Frank the attendant, is con-stant vigilance.

I walk to my car, which is legally parked with plastic tag correctly displayed, and am about to get in when I notice a great cloud of smoke in the car next to mine.

Knock, knock. I tap on the driver's window. A face press-ing close to the glass emerges from the cloud. It is Chug Van Duzer.

"Yo, it's the cops," Chug says to his buddies. Lots of bustling inside the car.

Knock, knock. "Chug, you wanna roll down the window, please?"

Chug rolls down the window. "Yeah, man. What can I do you for, Mr. Nay-ring?" Cough, cough.

"Well, for starters, you and your buddies can refrain from smoking what I'll assume is tobacco in your car. I seem to remember something about school rules forbidding that."

"Oh, man. We just wanted a little change of scenery, you know."

"Listen, Chug, you and your buddies pack up right now and head inside. I won't say anything about this."

"Deal," says Chug. "Let's go, guys." Four doors fly open and six guys, all of whom I recognize from the smoking area, tumble out amid coughing and sniffling, slam the doors, and take off for the school entrance.

"Later, dude," says Chug. All of a sudden I feel had. Chug et al were awful quick to accept my "deal."

I climb in my car and head for the bank, two miles down Hudson Avenue, Amesley's main street.

Amesley is no great shakes, though residents like to think otherwise. It is essentially a small-town community that suffers from delusions of suburban grandeur. The town council, as well as the dominant merchants and business people, all bear familiar Amesley names and live in the older parts of town built up during the 1920s and 1930s. They are staunch Republicans. Newcomers, state bureaucrats, university professors, hospital employees, and office workers live in the newer developments, tend to vote Democrat, and use fertilizer on their lawns, which gives Amesley its suburban feel. Historically, residents tend to "support" education, which means that they usually vote yes on the school budget. But school officials have charted a prudent course of modest tax increases each year in order to slowly expand programs without raising red flags that might provoke concerned-citizen groups into tax-reform campaigns.

A few years ago Laurie (Mrs. Nehring) and I left the city

and bought a house in Amesley. We did so for all the usual
reasons that people leave cities and move to suburbs. Safe
neighborhoods, good schools (everything's relative), and rising property values. We bought in an older neighborhood,
but we vote Democrat and use fertilizer—although it does
not turn our lawn green. When we were considering the
move to Amesley, everyone gave us free advice on living
in the same town where you teach. Well, it's okay as long
as you're in the good graces of everyone in the community,
but just see what happens when you fail your neighbor's
kid. Living in Amesley's all right, as long as you don't mind
being watched every time you go to the supermarket or
drink a beer on your back porch. The underlying theme of
all these sage comments was *don't do it*. But we liked the
house and the neighborhood.

So we did it. All in all, it's worked out pretty well.
Mostly encounters with students outside of school are
positive. Especially with kids that have reputations as
troublemakers at school. Allen Karimosov, frequent
smoker in boys' room and picker of fights, lives two blocks
away. In school he's a terror. Teachers tell me he's continually disruptive in class, refuses to do work, and all the
rest. From my daily tour of duty in ISS, I know that he's
often there, as often as the best of them. After raising hell
at school, Allen spends his afternoons doing yard work
around the neighborhood. We see each other from time
to time and wave. He mows the Jessups' lawn next door.
One hot day last July he was working up a real sweat over
at the Jessups', pushing and pulling the mower around
flower beds and shrubberies, when the engine quit. He
couldn't get it started and was looking pretty bothered.
I brought over a glass of lemonade.

"I thought you could use a break."

"Oh, gee, Mr. Nehring, thanks a lot." Allen downs the lemonade in one long draft and hands back the glass.

"You're workin' pretty hard over here," I say.

"Yeah, I gotta do three more lawns this morning, but the damn mower quit."

"How many customers do you have, Allen?"

"I don't know. I guess maybe twenty or twenty-five."

"Wow. Do you charge by the hour?"

"No. They pay by the job. I give 'em an estimate based on how big the lawn is, and then they pay for every time I do it."

"You must do pretty well."

"I do all right. I'm gonna get a truck pretty soon."

"Sounds good. Well, more power to you. I'll let you get back to your mower."

"Thanks for the lemonade, Mr. Nehring."

"Anytime."

I felt like I could invite Allen over for a beer and we could sit on the back patio and shoot the breeze. He seemed like a nice kid, with interests, goals, drive—all the things we like at school.

Then there's Ed Parker. Ed failed English Eleven—*my* English Eleven—and has a reputation as a druggie at school. He never caused me any grief in class, but judging by his demeanor on most days, I'd say his reputation was deserved. I'd see Ed around the neighborhood riding his bicycle. Usually he'd smile and wave. Once he smiled and gave me the finger. I think that was right after final report cards came out. But next time it was back to smile and wave. I was talking to Mrs. Carnahan across the street one day. She's older, a widow, and lives alone.

"Do you know Eddie Parker at school, Jim?" she asked.

"Yes, I do," I answered, figuring it's safer to withhold

any editorial comment. Who knows, the kid could be her grandnephew.

"I bet he's a fine student. You know, he does my house-keeping, and on my birthday last month he brought me a bouquet of flowers. He's such a dear."

"Yeah, he's a nice boy, Mrs. Carnahan."

I guess school just brings out the worst in all of us.

But I've been fortunate. My house has never been vandalized, and I've never been the target of obscene phone calls. Aaron Rosenblum, earth-science teacher, who also lives in Amesley, has been so victimized. One Halloween night Aaron was awakened by a loud crash downstairs. He found his living-room window broken and on the living-room floor among the glass shards was a fist-size chunk of scrap metal with a note taped to it. The note said, "Fuck you, Aaron." Well, that was not the end of it. For the next several weeks phone calls came into the house about every other day, all with the same mes-sage. Then about a month later another chunk of metal came through the newly replaced window with the same taped-on message. At this point Aaron, with the assistance of George Handelman and Ralph Peters, put two and two together. They had Aaron make up a list of all the kids he thought might do such a thing and found out that one of the kids on the list worked in a machine shop near Aaron's house and certainly had access to pieces of scrap metal to which abusive notes might be taped and hurled through living-room windows. They were all about to haul the kid in when out of the blue the kid's parents called the school and requested a conference with Mr. Peters, Mr. Handelman, Mr. Rosenblum, and the kid, whose name was Harold Malloy. All met. Parents and kid mutually exclaimed how sorry they were and how it was a malicious and wicked act, and a check was handed over, which more than covered the expense of the two windows, and everything seemed pretty copacetic.

Then Aaron said it wasn't enough, that he was going to contact the district attorney and press charges, what charges he was not quite sure, but by golly, he was gonna get that kid but good. Teach the community a lesson. Then Aaron said that what really upset him was not the rocks or the obscene phone calls but the swastika that had been etched on his aluminum siding by what looked to have been the rough end of a piece of scrap metal, indeed the sort of a piece of scrap metal that one might obtain from the discard bin in a machine shop. That was the first time that anyone had heard about the swastika. Harold confessed then and there. There was much gasping. Aaron said to expect a phone call and then walked out.

Much phone calling, letter writing, apologizing, and general head shaking ensued. The upshot was that the parents said, well, if this teacher was going to really prosecute with the DA and all, then, by golly, they were going to sue the district for inducing such a state of emotional agony in their son that he would turn to violent and deranged acts. The DA stalled, the school officials worked to soothe tempers while at the same time keeping the whole thing out of the papers, and eventually it all fizzled out. Aaron quit teaching two years later. He remodels houses now and says he's much happier.

I check my watch. It is 1:10. I have twenty-seven minutes. I don't think I'm gonna make it in time. I shouldn't have stopped to listen to Ethel Port recite Langston Hughes. But I'm at the bank, and the line doesn't look too long. I walk in, get in line. There, standing in front of me, is Alice Ronald. Mrs. Ronald turns, sees me, smiles, says, "Well, hello, Mr. Nehring." I can see it in her eyes: Mrs. Ronald wants to talk about her son, Ronald—I mean, Michael—

right then and there in that line with all those people in clear earshot.

Mrs. Ronald winds up for the pitch and . . . "How's Michael doing in class these days?"

"Oh, he's doing all right." I scramble to recall without the aid of notes or plan book how one Michael Ronald is doing in English, or is it social studies? No, English. Suddenly I seem to remember that he has not turned in his research proposal, due last week.

I say, "There are some specifics we could talk about, though. How about I call you tonight?"

Mrs. Ronald says, "Oh, I don't mind discussing it here. Besides, you'd probably never catch me in. I'm always running here and there. How's he doing?"

"He hasn't turned in his research proposal. It was due last week. It's an important part of a major assignment." I hope I'm right.

"Gee, I wish you'd told me sooner. I'll get after him right away, Mr. Nehring. Anything else?"

"No. Otherwise he's doing fine." We make small talk about the weather and how the air-conditioning must be on in the bank because the lobby is so cold.

Would a normal, educated person ever ask for a medical consult in the middle of a bank lobby? Well, Mrs. Ronald, we ran that test on your stool sample and everything checks out but we're still concerned about those hemorrhoids that just won't go away—it's been eighteen months. What if I'd told Mrs. Ronald that I thought her son was misplaced and belonged in the slow class, and that his IQ was below average, or that I was concerned because he showed signs of child abuse? Would that have been "okay" for everybody in the bank lobby to hear?

I do my bank business and leave for school. It's 1:30 P.M.

I have seven minutes—twelve minutes, actually—until I'm plain late.

Talking with Mrs. Ronald makes me think about parents, and that makes me think about Amy Cranston. Amy was very bright, maybe one of the brightest kids at Amesley. Not only was she bright but she was interested and she worked. She was intellectually voracious. She could do anything. I used to kid with Laurie that Amy Cranston was a human word processor. I'd give her an assignment, tell her a due date, and with no further discussion she would deliver on or before the date due a letter-perfect product. No matter what I gave her, she could do it. Her research paper—I had her in English Eleven—was masterful. While other kids struggled with the card catalog, Amy was off interviewing the entire political science department at the state university. Her research dealt with the ways in which public officials have assigned the label "terrorist" in order to shape public policy, all of which she beautifully summarized in her conclusion, pointing out that the only real difference between a freedom fighter and a terrorist is which side one is on.

So Amy got an A+ on her paper, as she got on most everything else, and that was that. Except that Amy's parents felt it wasn't enough.

"We feel Amy is not being challenged enough," said Mrs. Cranston when she called sometime during the second quarter.

"Why is that?" I answered.

"Well, she's got an average in the high nineties in almost all her courses."

"Uh-huh," I said.

"Well, we just feel she could be doing more," said Mrs. Cranston. Thus Mrs. Cranston said much about how Amy could be doing more homework because on Tuesday and Thursday evenings she had no lessons or other commitments and there were two good blocks of time for her to work, and how she was Harvard-bound, didn't I know, and she already had scored 1200 on the SATs in seventh grade, and I said "Uh-huh" at the appropriate moments, and the conversation eventually just sort of ran down and we hung up. Next day in my mailbox I received a note from the guidance office requesting my presence at a case conference for Amy Cranston. Amy's parents, the note informed me, would be present, along with Amy and all her teachers.

Case conferences are interesting happenings. That puts it mildly. Actually there is usually deep apprehension all the way around. Everybody feels extremely vulnerable. First, the kid. The kid is surrounded by adults, who under normal circumstances are disapproving of youth in general but in this special instance may concentrate their collective gripes on one individual. This much the kid knows and feels. What the kid doesn't know is that he or she is also the most likely scapegoat among those present, when the moment comes for assignment of blame. He or she will become the handy diversion for irresponsible behavior, neglect, or missed opportunities on the part of the adults, who between disapproving remarks will condescend to say how this is all for the kid's sake, after all, and how none of them would be here if they didn't care about the kid and all the rest, which the kid recognizes is suspect at best.

Then there's the teacher. The teacher arrives trying to think of some small bit of real knowledge that he or she may possess about the kid's academic ability, character, learning style, personality, etc., such that this small bit of knowledge may be shared with the group in order to create the illusion that the teacher knows the kid, when in fact most people at the conference—the other teachers, the guidance counselor, and the kid—know that this is clearly untrue. Having considered and perhaps landed upon some small bit of non-knowledge, the teacher will still feel intense apprehension at the possibility of being accused of not having done enough for the kid. This is especially troublesome because, if accused, the teacher will feel guilty in one hundred percent of all cases, so deep is the sense of professional guilt. A stated or implied accusation during the conference will only make everyone more acutely mindful of this fact, especially the teacher, who arrives at the meeting fearing that it will happen to him or her. As a desperate stay against utter nervous collapse, the teacher will arrive with the only non-knowledge acceptable to everyone, the only exchangeable currency of the institution: grades.

Third is the guidance counselor. Like the teacher, the guidance counselor arrives with an acute sense of ignorance about the individual who is the focus of this meeting, and who, professionally, is the object of the collective labors of the assembled educators (and about whom all the educators collectively know not a whit except for *the grades*, which are greatly talked about only to the extent that they are deeply meaningless). The counselor faces an even more awesome abyss of ignorance because whereas each teacher has direct responsibility for maybe one hundred and twenty-five students, the counselor is likely responsible for the "counseling" of about three hundred and fifty. (That is possibly one of the most laughable facts of a laughable institution—if one finds any of this humorous.) The guidance counselor might more aptly be called a schedule manager, since managing schedules is all one may realistically do for three hundred and fifty kids.

Finally come the parents, no less vulnerable than anyone else in the group: after all, they are *the kid's parents*. If the kid's rotten, it's their fault, or so the parents fear everyone else at the conference will see it. Indeed, the parents may see it this way themselves. In addition, they are bewildered. They do not understand what happened to the cute kid they knew in elementary school and junior high. The kid who dressed up nice and sang in the school chorus, who simmered down when you said simmer down, who was full of benign energy, who smiled and laughed and didn't cause nobody no trouble. Suddenly the cute kid is no longer a kid but an adult—a kind of weird, unapproachable adult with odd clothes and odd manners. Not the sort of adult that you meet in the office or the supermarket. What to do? Send him to school and hope maybe those educators can straighten the kid out. Only that begs the question of where did the kid pick up all those odd manners and odd clothes? Answer: school?

Thus we find ourselves—kid, teachers, guidance counselor, and parents—seated in Conference Room 3 around a big table for the Amy Cranston Case Conference. Nobody says a word. Bernice Fleischman stifles a sneeze, whispers, "Excuse me." We are waiting for Joe Grossi, math teacher. Finally Alex, Amy's guidance counselor, who has been shuffling papers in Amy's folder, says, "Well, I guess we should begin.

"We're here this afternoon to assess the appropriateness of Amy's present schedule and see what changes might possibly be made. I suppose the best way to begin is for each of Amy's teachers to give a brief rundown as far as what they see in Amy's situation." Here followed brief rundowns, rundowns mostly of grades on tests and assignments plus averages. The rundowns were peppered

lightly with anecdotes intended to demonstrate insight into
Amy's character. Bernice mentioned how Amy must have
some good German blood in her, and Joe, who finally
arrived all smiles and apologies, said that Amy was the
only one of his students to earn a 100 on the recent unit
test. I said how from what I knew that I thought Amy
seemed well adjusted, happy, and was doing well
academically—so why argue with success? Then I said,
"Why don't we ask Amy?" She had been sitting quietly,
occupying as little space as possible at one end of the table.
So I asked Amy if she felt challenged and successful and
working to her fullest abilities, to which Amy answered
a hesitant yes, and Mrs. Cranston winced. Mr. Cranston
remained generally stoic.

Then it was the Cranstons' turn to speak. Mrs. Cranston
said (again) how she and Mr. Cranston—she looked at Mr.
Cranston, who attempted a smile—felt that Amy was not
being challenged by her teachers. She didn't say courses;
she definitely said teachers. At that there was a silent,
collective huff among the assembled educators. No one
heard it, but all of us felt it and suddenly felt also that
we were all on the same side and now we knew who the
enemy was. First, Mrs. Cranston turned to Tony Desista,
Amy's chemistry teacher, and said couldn't Mr. Desista
come up with some special projects for Amy over and
above the required curriculum? At that, Amy harrumphed
and Tony said well, sure, but he would not be able to
take class time to work with Amy on them because of the
other twenty-odd kids in the class. A similar dialogue ensued between Mrs. Cranston and Bernice. The lines were
drawn.

My turn was next. I said likewise, adding that because
Amy excels above her peers, she often takes leadership

roles in group activities and in effect tutors her classmates and how that's certainly a valuable activity in and
of itself and how school is not just a place to earn high
grades but a place to gain valuable social skills and certain
qualities of character like compassion, and how I could
see Amy was developing all those things. I'm afraid I
sounded too preachy, because Mrs. Cranston just sort of
said uh-huh and turned quickly to the next teacher. Eventually we all agreed that we would "look into ways" in
which we, in our various subjects, might challenge Amy
more, and the Cranstons said thank you and everybody
shook hands and left and nothing changed, and within
three weeks everyone had more or less forgotten the Amy
Cranston conference.

Why did nothing change? Because teachers teach courses,
not students. When a teacher sits down in August to plan
out the coming year, he or she does not make copious notes
on the students he will have. He can't because he does not
know who they will be; he probably never met ninety percent of them. In addition, there will be over a hundred of
them, anyway, so "copious notes" would mean a book-
length manuscript. No, the teacher sits down and plans out
what content will be covered in his course. The year begins,
the course is taught, and all students must in lockstep fashion proceed through the material at the predetermined pace,
in the predetermined manner. If a kid works slower than
the predetermined pace, he "fails"; if he works faster, he
gets bored; if he doesn't connect with the monolithic method
of instruction, he gets confused. In all three situations a
case conference may be convened. Much is said, little is
done. Little *can* be done. Thinks the teacher, How in hell
can I individualize instruction when I have a hundred and
thirty-five kids and we've got to cover all this material? Get
in step, kid, or "fail."

* * *

I pull into the Amesley High parking lot. Incredibly, my parking space has not been taken. I nab it. 1:35 P.M. I'm in good shape. I walk into the building, by the main office, by the library, by the smoking area, by the cafeteria. Whoa! In the cafeteria a game of soda-can soccer is under way. In one corner of the room, tables have been pushed aside and a group of three boys defends their goal—the space between two wall vents—against another team of three. All six are kicking wildly at close range. Suddenly the defending goalie gets a clear shot and the crushed soda can goes skidding across the floor and pings against a metal table leg at the other end of the cafeteria. A cheer goes up from the defending team. Mr. Nehring steps in.

"Ah, excuse me, guys. I'm glad you're all having a good time, but could I say something? People generally don't eat lunch in the middle of a soccer game because it would be sort of dangerous, right? Now, by the same token, people generally don't play soccer in the middle of a cafeteria because that's dangerous, too, right? Do you get my drift?

"Yeah, we get your drift."

"Good. Would you please put the tables back too."

"No problem, dude."

"Thank you."

The cafeteria is alive with teenagers—C lunch, last lunch of the day. The area shows the usual signs of wear and tear for this time of day: garbage cans filled to overflowing, scraps of food scattered about the floor, tables askew. The lunch ladies, who look harried at the beginning of the day, are now looking like they will strangle the next kid who hands them a folded dollar or a large bill. Though the room resembles a war zone shortly after armistice, the damage is

largely superficial (excepting the damage to the lunch ladies), and by tomorrow morning the place will be restored
and ready for another four rounds of lunch. The chaos is
generally benign.

With certain exceptions. Several years ago I had lunch
duty (an assignment since negotiated out of the teachers'
contract) when one day B lunch erupted into a food fight.
There had been rumors earlier that day. I'd heard a kid in
third-period social studies say something under his breath
about the table near the exit and Jason Long and cubed
Jell-O. I shared this piece of intelligence with Tony Desista,
my duty partner, at the beginning of lunch. Tony said he'd
heard similar rumors, only it was about those government-
surplus peanuts they sell in little paper cups, and in addition
to Jason Long, Billy Riegel and Michael Madison were
somehow involved. Tony and I were on the lookout. Near
the end of B lunch, Jason Long and Michael Madison got
up from where they were seated near the ice-cream freezer
and moved over to the table by the exit. I gave Tony the
eye and pointed. We both started nonchalantly toward that
table by the exit.

Suddenly I was aware of some big commotion behind
me. I turned and saw two tables full of kids at opposite
sides of the cafeteria standing at their places hurling Jell-O
cubes and peanuts at each other. For the most part, the
Jell-O cubes and the peanuts reached their targets or the
wall beyond—which shortly became plastered with red-
and-green Jell-O smears. Of course, not everybody's aim
was one hundred percent accurate and not everybody had
the kind of throwing arm that one hundred percent of the
time could propel the chosen object the full length of the
selected distance, which is to say that some of the people
in between the warring parties got hit and stood up, saying
something like, "Hey, what's the big idea?" and immedi-

ately got pummeled with peanuts and red-and-green Jell-O cubes, to which they quickly responded in kind by grabbing all available ammunition from the lunch trays in the vicinity and hurling it in several directions. This in turn meant that additional innocent bystanders got hit, who in turn responded in kind, and pretty soon the air was filled with flying Jell-O cubes and surplus peanuts plus an occasional dinner roll and other throwable items that had to suffice once the supply of Jell-O cubes and peanuts was exhausted.

It was quite a scene. A real massacre. Defenseless children scattering in every direction, peace lovers caught in the cross fire, eager recruits boldly firing from atop exposed tabletops and getting hit, soldiers scouring the floor for reusable ammo, the wounded retreating and inspecting the damage, and the lunch ladies hiding behind their cash registers. Jason Long, Michael Madison, and Billy Riegel didn't lift a finger the whole time. They just watched—the generals, I guess. The whole battle lasted about two minutes, and just as it was running down, the bell rang. This was fortuitous because at the bell everyone headed for the exit, innocent and guilty alike. Only Tony and I had stationed ourselves at the only non-emergency exits from the room and stood, arms outstretched, feet planted firmly, ready to stop the thundering herd. They stopped. Thank goodness.

"Have a seat, everyone!" we were yelling.

There was much mumbling, some pleading: "But I didn't have anything to do with it, you gonna punish everybody for something just a few kids did?" But ultimately there was compliance. We controlled the exit. The room slowly got sort of cleaned up, mostly by persons who had nothing to do with the food fight but were just anxious to get to class because they knew they'd get in trouble for being late, and saying how Mr. Desista and Mr. Nehring kept them late would not get them out of it because then the teacher would say, so why did Mr. Desista and Mr. Nehring keep them late, and they'd say for something we didn't do, and the teacher would say uh-huh in that tone of voice that means "I don't believe you." The kids who had been fighting mostly stood near the exit and watched everybody else clean up. They didn't care about being late. It was all pretty unfair. I felt like a petty dictator, but I was also mad at the kids who'd started it. I considered making a starving-children-in-Africa speech but decided against it because, even though it might be very apropos, nobody would listen; it would all be just lots of preachy adult talk, and that made me even angrier that these kids wouldn't appreciate hunger and famine, and they think it's funny to just throw food around and mess up the cafeteria. Middle-class ennui, I thought to myself. That helped a little.

The soda-can soccer game stops. Soccer players put the tables back in place, and I turn to leave the cafeteria on my way to English Eleven, Slow. As I head down the hallway the bell rings. The hall fills with kids. Kids pouring out of classrooms up and down the hall. Kids pouring out of the cafeteria. Kids pouring out of adjoining hallways. This is really very liquid. I think of those speeded-up, time-lapse movies taken from the tops of buildings, looking down on swarms of cars and pedestrians racing this way and that. Somebody ought to make one of those of Amesley High sometime. Those movies always make people look so ridiculous. Rushing here and there, then rushing right back. Stop and start, back and forth. Not that they really aren't ridiculous. Because really, they really are. The movie just makes it plain.

Which is to say I'm pretty ridiculous because here I am caught in the midst of it, midstream in the main office hallway sailing down to Room 25.

Two nicely dressed boys, sophomores, come into earshot in front of me. I follow them. They don't know a teacher is right behind them.

"He was doin' bongs or somethin' upstairs. And they had a keg in the basement. That's where everybody was. Everybody was like totally wasted. Stacey Damcek got so drunk, she started taking her shirt off."

"You're kidding," says the other kid.

"No, really. It was wicked funny. And everybody was just like falling all over the place. It was generally pretty funny except that Alec Pointe threw up all over the coffee table, like all in the corn chips and everything. It looked like nacho sauce. It was pretty gross."

"Oh, gross."

"But they say he was like tripping on LSD and that's why he threw up because he was like drinking beer at the same time and I wouldn't be surprised if he'd like been upstairs doing bongs, you know. I mean, Alec's pretty radical."

Just another Saturday night in Amesley. From what I hear (overhear mostly), the drug scene, including alcohol, is alive and deadly at Amesley. In the last month I've heard kids mention or allude to beer, booze, LSD, marijuana, cocaine, heroin, crack, and pills of an undisclosed nature. The talk generally revolves around local parties at which the above items are available, or friends who have access to or make use of the same. Beer and booze seem to be the most prevalent, I guess because they are easiest to obtain and carry the mildest legal and parental caveat. Marijuana, which seemed to be the drug of choice when I was growing up, has fallen out of favor, maybe because it's so plentiful and cocaine is so much more chic. Anyway, they're all there and they're all used.

What of it? It's hard to say really why kids do drugs. I guess most of the reasons I've heard apply in some cases. Kids do drugs because kids by nature are adventurous and don't consider consequences (sometimes even flying kites off hundred-fifty-foot cliffs) and because the drugs are accessible. Kids do drugs because more now than ever there's not some responsible grown-up within earshot to stop them. Kids do drugs because they experience acute social pressures like divorce, peer competition, school demands. Kids do drugs because of middle-class ennui (there it is again). Kids do drugs because they don't see anything better to do. Kids do drugs because drugs are available.

How do we deal with drugs at school? A few years back, drugs were standing center stage in the district. There'd been a fire at one of the elementary schools, and come to find out the kid who started it was found to be carrying a bag of cocaine. This was reported in the local paper, and the next week local TV sent a reporter and camera crew to do a piece on drugs in the suburbs. The piece aired a week later on the six-o'clock news, and pretty soon the superintendent's phone was ringing off the hook. A committee was convened to "look into the problem." About the only memorable thing that came out of the committee was an anti-drug slogan for which the committee had sponsored a contest. The winning entry was "Don't do drugs!" which I guess the committee felt was direct and therefore clearly understandable by all. The slogan soon appeared on buttons that staff members were encouraged to wear, banners that were spread across entrance foyers, and student-designed posters hung in hallways and classrooms. A month later I don't think a single faculty member could be found wearing the button, and most probably did not know what had become of it, anyway. The banner that hung in the main office foyer was sagging very low and then one day was just not there anymore. And the white space around the hallway and classroom posters started to fill with graffiti. One artist had made an effort to get as many posters in the high school as possible so that before the posters eventually came down, about two thirds of them read, "Don't do drugs, do beer." (What the kid lacked in creativity, he made up for in effort.)

The next year, district administrators decided to have a Drug Awareness Day, during which all district students, kindergarten through twelfth grade, would participate in informational seminars and peer discussions and other drug-awareness activities. At the high school an assembly was held to which a very large, weighty National Football League star was invited to impress upon the kids that you can become famous and make lots of money without the aid of drugs, and that experimenting with drugs is danger-ous. This person was all the talk around school for the next few days, and there seemed to be a kind of resurgence of Amesley football spirit.

Drug Awareness Day may have made kids more *aware* of drugs, but it did not seem to curb drug use. At least that's what Dick Brown said.

Dick Brown is Amesley's on-staff social worker. It's Dick's job to step into the breach between the school's pre-sumed responsibility to respond to kids' personal needs, and the school's inability to do so. Between the guidance counselor's race to get his three hundred and fifty kids' schedules worked out and the teacher's maniacal disposition toward covering content, there are plenty of troubled kids whose troubles do not get noticed. Apparently they don't get noticed at home, either. Anyway, Dick said that for about a week after Drug Awareness Day he had a very full schedule of counseling with kids who for the moment put aside talk of problems with parents, teachers, girlfriends, and boyfriends, and talked exclusively about drugs. Then, says Dick, after about a week everything went back to normal. For Dick, normal means a full range of crises rather than just one kind.

In addition to Amesley's sporadic and public displays of "concern" over drugs, there are day-to-day efforts to deal with the problem.

Ellie Grosshartig is Amesley's health teacher. For years Ellie has been teaching kids about sexuality, personal hygiene, nutrition, drugs and alcohol, family life, peer relationships, and other matters of very immediate concern to high-school-age kids. She answers kids' questions honestly and intelligently. She addresses health topics with an eye toward meeting the needs of her students and an eye toward scholarly treatment of the subject, drawing on research in psychology, human physiology, and other hard disciplines. Kids come away with a better sense of who they are and a deepened curiosity about academic subjects.

Ellie works at avoiding the spotlight, which gets turned her way anytime sex education or drugs or suicide or the like is played up in the media. Fortunately for Ellie, Dick Brown has an outgoing and aggressive personality and usually steps in to speak for the school. That means Ellie can keep doing her quiet work quietly. Ellie says she prefers to avoid public attention because the kind of sporadic public outcry over health-related issues inevitably results in a knee-jerk response by the schools. Committees look into the problem, slogans are recited, and special days get organized. All to little avail. Ellie calls these kinds of happenings "mowing down the weeds." Every so often, she says, the weeds get too high for suburban taste and the schools get asked to mow them down. By the time they start to grow back, a few days later, the public is looking the other way. Ellie is not bitter about this fact, but she is savvy and professional enough to recognize it and to work in spite of it.

Ellie says that drug and alcohol abuse, along with suicide and other social pathologies, are only the symptoms of deeper problems in our culture. We are too strongly motivated by ambition and not service, says Ellie. As a society, we have too little cohesion because of our deep affection for individuality and free enterprise. And we search for comfortable surroundings where we should search for love. The symptoms start to appear, she says, because ambition fades, loneliness eventually closes in, and loveless comforts fail to nurture.

8.

The School of Athens

• • •

Ellie's right, I think. And because she's right, the business of schooling is very, very important indeed. It's worth your tax dollars, and it's worth the best efforts of the best minds to make school a place of nurture and growth, a place seriously engaged in the work of positive social transformation.

My last-period class is called English Eleven S. S stands for Slow. I guess by calling it S, we school people hope to disguise the fact that we consider the kids in the class to be what the S stands for. We do not want to stigmatize them. Of course, if we were really concerned about stigma, then we wouldn't have segregated the 5 percent of each grade level that make up the slow classes from the 95 percent who are mainstreamed and "heterogenified" and nontracked and nonstigmatized, regardless of whether we attach to the group the letter *S* or the word *slow*. The label is not the stigma. The fact of the class is.

There are eleven students enrolled in English Eleven S. They are Esther Paige, Jay Carlozzi, Tammy Rutger, Dawn Jenko, Brian Hann, Donny Trowbridge, Alexis Lesandre, Rosemary Montana, Todd Lopez, Rebecca Thornton, and Terry Hueber. More than in my other classes, I feel I know these kids. They are individuals with personalities that emerge in our classroom activities, since, after all, there are only twelve of us. I guess it works both ways. My personality shows more as well, because I can interact with them on an individual basis. Consequently we have a good rapport, we get along, we are a group. Whereas most years I have dreaded my last-period class because social studies or English is usually the furthest thing from a kid's mind at that time of day, I look forward to meeting with this group. They are spunky, relaxed, a little unruly, but, because of their numbers, manageable.

Jay Carlozzi walks into the room. He's almost always the first one to arrive. And he always wants to know what Mr. Nehring has planned for the day. I'm straightening papers at my desk and Jay walks in. He spots a TV sitting on a cart in one corner of the room.

"Missah Nehring, we seein' a filmsrip aday?" Jay slurs his words and regards certain sounds (such as *t*) as unimportant, so he usually leaves them out. In addition, his opening question, and he always has one, is usually an impossible question because there is a misunderstanding or wrong assumption embedded in it—akin to the old line, "When did you stop beating your spouse?" I always wonder whether I should give Jay a straight answer or attempt to disclose the fallacy in his question. Today's fallacy is that the TV will be used to project a filmstrip.

"Ah, no, we—"

"Then how come 'ere's a TV in a room?"

"Well, because Mrs. Arturo from AV brought it up for Mrs. Stewart next door, but Mrs. Stewart wasn't in, and Mrs. Arturo didn't have a key to the room, so she asked if she could leave the TV in my room."

"How come you said we couldn' see a filmsrip yesaday?"

"I said you couldn't see a videotape."

"Whaever, but 'ere's a TV in a room so let's see a filmsrip or a video or whaever."

"Well, I didn't plan to show one today, because we weren't scheduled to get a TV."

"Yeah, bu' 'ere's one sandin' righ' 'ere, so le's see a filmsrip."

"Yes, but that's for Mrs. Stewart."

"Yeah, bu' Mrs. Sewar ain' here."

"Yes, but we don't know when she might all of a sudden appear and want her TV, and besides that, we're going to have a discussion today."

"So how bou' afer a discussion?"

"Well, I don't have the videotape with me."

"So how are we gonna see a filmsrip? You said we were gonna see one. You lied."

"No, Jay. I didn't lie. We're scheduled to get a TV tomorrow, and that's when we're going to see the video."

"You know, Missah Nehrin', you don' make no sense aday."

"What can I say, Jay? I guess it's a hazard of the profession."

"I guess so. 'a's cool, oh."

"Thanks, Jay. Listen, could you give me a hand with these desks?" I don't think I've ever had a conversation with Jay that wasn't in some way out of joint.

For today's discussion, twelve desks must be pulled out of their columns and rows and placed in a circle. Today we're discussing a story called "The End," which is narrated by a Japanese boy dying of radiation poisoning in 1945. He reflects on the bombing of Hiroshima, the source of his disease. The editors of the anthology in which "The End" appears include with the story information about President Truman's decision to use the atom bomb, and statistics showing lives lost and projected casualties (according to the

U.S. Army) had the bomb not been used. Yesterday students spent the second half of the period reading the story as I passed among them, helping with vocabulary and difficult passages. Today they will take ten minutes to complete ten multiple-choice questions about the story. Then we will proceed with a round-table discussion based on a single question: Do you think it was right for the United States to drop the bomb on Hiroshima?

I'm a little nervous because the success of the class depends on their willingness to deal extemporaneously with that question. I haven't really planned any backup activities that can occupy remaining minutes should the discussion fail to last to the end of the period. This lack of a contingency plan goes against common sense and everything I was always taught in education courses—(Always have a contingency plan!)—but it's intentional. I want to put myself and my students to the acid test, to force us to wrestle with the question—to force me to wrestle with the dynamics of discussion leading. Although I have no contingency plan, I have done everything that I reasonably may to ensure that the discussion is a success. I have chosen a story at an appropriate reading level. I have ensured that students read the story, in this case by allowing time in class. I have coached students to ensure that they not only passed their eyes over the words but also understood them. I have chosen a question for which there is no easy answer and over which there is a very good chance of disagreement (ergo, a discussion). I have arranged the class physically in such a way that all may address the group and all are equally exposed and all are represented as equals in the circle—I sit at a student desk along with everybody else. In addition to my physical equality with the group, I will attempt to establish my intellectual presence as that of an equal by laying low in the discussion and trying as much as possible to encourage back and forth among the students. Finally, to ensure success, I have labored through the year to establish a climate in the room of respect for all persons and opinions. Which is all to say that short of having that contingency plan—a handy little map exercise or workbook activity dittoed off and ready to be handed out—I've done everything possible to ensure success. But I'm still nervous.

Why am I nervous? Because try as I may, I cannot exercise complete control over what goes on in my classroom. The nature of teaching never allows that. Besides me, there will be a classful of other independently thinking and acting individuals in the room over whom I never have absolute control.

The gap between my efforts to take control and my inability to do so is a big part of what gives teaching its interest. During each class I fly into the air, not really knowing which way the wind will blow, relying on my skill to respond to the unpredictable updrafts, downdrafts, sudden gusts, and squalls. It's a thrill. And today there are no parachutes on board.

Alexis Lesandre walks in. Bleached blond hair, long red fingernails, heavy (false?) eyelashes, raspy voice, and a well-developed smoker's cough. Alexis enters coughing. Rosemary Montana is right behind. Rosemary is robust, buxom, and sweetly pugnacious. She's popular with the guys in the class and knows it. Her way of saying hi to any one of them is to punch him hard in the shoulder, smile mischievously, and say, "Hey, dude, how's it hangin'?"

Right behind Rosemary is Todd Lopez, who sneaks up behind Rosemary and tickles her under the ribs.

"Hey, scumbag, what's your problem?" says Rosemary in customary parlance, by which Rosemary does not mean offense and to which Todd does not take offense.

"Yo, mama," says Todd. "I didn't do nothin'."

Tammy Rutger, Brian Hann, and Esther Paige burst through the doorway in an uproar of laughter.

"What's so funny, guys?" I ask.

"Mr. Nehring, you wouldn't believe it," says Brian.

"What's that, Brian?"

"Don't tell Mr. Nehring, Brian," says Tammy.

"No, go ahead, tell him, he's cool," says Esther.

"What is it, Brian?" I'm interested.

"Well, there was this guy in the hall just now, and well, he was a rather"—Brian attempts discretion—"he was a rather large individual, and he had on this short T-shirt and jeans, and his jeans were like way down low so that from the back it looked like half his butt was hangin' out."

"And it was all hairy too," adds Tammy. Another uproar of laughter. I can't help cracking a smile both at Brian's tale and Tammy's obvious shock at what she saw.

Jay and I finish arranging desks. The rest of the class arrives, with less flourish than the Tammy–Esther–Brian trio. I pick up a stack of file folders from the counter by the door and lay them out on the rearranged desks, one folder to a desk, one folder belonging to each student. Keeping a comprehensive folder for each student and holding the folder in the room offers a sense of security that the student will always begin class with the materials he or she needs that day. I'm not sure who feels more secure—the student for knowing he won't get hollered at, or me for not having to holler and get my blood pressure up. At any rate, the folder routine works pretty well, so I keep with it. (The folder idea is what remains of my first-year attempt to impose order and structure on an unruly class and exemplifies a kind of natural selection that takes place in teaching. The fittest ideas survive and the weak ones get omitted next time through.)

Aside from the bit about security, the folders offer a

chance for each kid to show off his personality. Brian's folder has big marijuana leaves on the front and back covers. The leaves have been drawn with obvious care, probably during lapses in attention to whatever it was Mr. Nehring was trying to teach. Now that all veins and tendrils have been sketched in, the only recent improvements have been to ink over some of the more important outlines or to embark on separate, but related, works in the remaining white space around the edges of each cover. In the lower right corner of the front cover Brian has neatly written in calligraphy, "It's a hard . . . it's a hard . . . it's a hard rain's a gonna fall." Under the quote, the name Jerry Garcia appears. I corrected Brian on this matter a few weeks ago, pointing out that though Jerry Garcia is responsible for many memorable lines, that one belongs to Bob Dylan. Brian said, "Oh, it doesn't matter," in a dismissive way that said he thought it probably did matter a great deal and that he was embarrassed that old Mr. Nehring knew more about teenage rebel culture than he, Brian, the teenage rebel.

"Why are the desks all funny, Mr. Nehring?" asks Rosemary.

Terry Hueber answers. "There's nothin' wrong with these desks. They're fine. What'sa matter with you, Rosie, huh? You high? You on drugs again? Mr. Nehring, Rosemary's on drugs again."

"Terry, Rosemary is not on drugs, but I'm beginning to wonder about you."

"Ooh," goes the class, finding their seats.

"Rosemary, the desks are all funny because we're having a discussion today."

"Oh, sick. That's cool." Rosemary approves.

"That's dumb. This is beat. How come we gotta move the desks around just to have a discussion?" asks Donny.

"Why do you think?" I ask.

"I don't know," says Donny. "If I knew, I would'n-a asked. Jesus." So much for Socratic method.

"Well, we don't *have* to move the desks around like this," I say, "but it's easier to talk to a bunch of people if you're facing them."

"That's dumb," says Donny.

"Okay, crew, have a seat where I've placed your folder. You've got a lot to do today, so we need to get started."

"Let's go, dudes," says Rosemary to Brian and Todd, who are fooling with my filmstrip projector in the back of the room. "Mr. Nehring wants your buns in these seats. Right, Mr. Nehring?"

"Something like that."

"Mr. Nehring wants my buns? What did you say, Rosie?"

"Cram it, Lopez," says Rosemary.

Brian and Todd laugh and take their seats. Brian nudges Donny, who is now facedown on his desk and looks asleep.

"Yo, shit for brains, wake up," says Brian.

"What the fuck, man?" Donny looks up, annoyed.

Brian backs off. "Hey, chill out. I didn't mean nothin'. The man wants to start class, is all."

This class communicates in ways that are noticeably different from my other classes, but all in all they are cohesive, frank, and humane. (Maybe more so than the others.) But they are tired. It is the end of the day—admittedly not yet two o'clock, but they've each been at this routine since seven-thirty this morning. They've been asked to "sit down" seven or eight times today, sat down for a good five hours total, and been ushered regularly to the next sit-down place with each bell. When you look at it that way, the routine of school appears as a kind of contest like flagpole sitting or marathon dancing. You spend so much time sitting or dancing with occasional short breaks until there's only one person left and he or she wins the contest. Only at school, the players who flag before the end of the day get sent to the principal's office.

We have kids from seven-thirty in the morning until about two or three in the afternoon. Essentially the community gives us custody of their sons and daughters for that amount of time and says do something educationally meaningful with them. Of course, they have certain expectations about what will go on during that time. Additionally there are state mandates that we must fulfill for required numbers of hours for certain activities and prescribed syllabi. But beyond that, we are more or less free to structure the experience of our students any way we please or, I should say, in a way that we believe would be most beneficial, most efficient, with the time we have. Despite this relative freedom almost every public high school in the United States divides time into forty-five-minute segments (or less), and doses out information mostly lecture-style in a daily rotation of discrete "subject-area" classes. I have tried to show in this book that although the conventional structure of public education may be said to "work" in some ways (most of them superficial), by and large it does not work *well*. So what, then, *does* work well? I don't know precisely, but I will offer some questions that may point in the general direction of a good answer.

How may we best engage kids? How may we best locate and exploit that point at which *their* interests and drives intersect with *our* educational aims—that point at which in the short run is called the lesson and in the long run we call curriculum? Answer: three more questions.

First, in what situations do we observe kids to be most engaged, in or out of school, for whatever reason? Here is a short list: smoking in boys' room; standing guard in front of boys' room; mowing lawns; fixing lawn mower; talking with peers in cafeteria; planning a cafeteria food fight; cruising the mall; watching a movie; playing a video game; putting on makeup; reading *Rolling Stone*; discussing the relative merits of popular songs, movies, music videos, and fashion; pursuing a relationship; analyzing relationships; playing baseball, football, soccer, tennis, softball, kick the can, freeze tag, and other sports that are voluntary; working on a car; working at McDonald's so that one may buy a car; SAT review sessions; final exams; making a videotape; rehearsing for a school play; taking photos for the school newspaper; writing an article for the school paper; working on the school literary magazine; working on the yearbook; AP classes; planning parties; some group activities in class; playing educational games and conducting simulations in class; some field trips; playing Hacky Sack; skateboarding; building a model airplane; biology dissections; making things in art class.

Second, what are the general characteristics of the above activities? Many of them are voluntary or involve voluntary participation to some degree. Many involve self-initiative. Some center on the making of a product; most involve extensive peer interaction. Some result in a kind of reward, either tangible or strongly intrinsic. Many involve elements of popular culture. Some focus on the building up of self-image. In some, people and personalities are the focus of an inquiry. Many involve a team or group working toward a goal. Many require cooperation and division of labor. Most are not under direct control of an adult. Some involve persons with similar interests. Some require persons of diverse interests. Many involve physical activity as a major component of the whole activity. Some involve competition and developing a strategy. In almost all there is a strong element of control that the individual has over the direction of the activity, the outcome, and his or her continued involvement in it. Many seek approval either by peers or by individuals more accomplished in the given activity. Almost all involve a sense of ownership and the pride of accomplishment. Many involve the resources of a school, but most inhabit realms outside of school either wholly or in part. Most involve periods of activity either less than or greater than forty-five minutes. Some commence unpredictably as interest rises, and stop as interest wanes. Some are bounded by strict time limits. Some rely on anxiety as a motivating factor. Many result in a performance, demonstration, or exhibit, or are in some way public activities. Most rely, for their continuation and shaping, on the individual responsiveness of those involved.

Third, what implications does all of this carry for the development of engaging, academically meaningful activity at school? That's a harder question to answer. It may be easier to begin by identifying those practices at school that would prevent or hinder students from becoming engaged. In our representative list above, there are relatively few activities that last exactly forty-five minutes, or which, for that matter, may be easily and regularly segmented into forty-five-minute allotments. Within the current structure of school, however, *all* activities must be so apportioned. There are also relatively few activities that are solitary, yet schoolwork more often than not is solitary work, whether it be listening to a lecture, completing a worksheet, watching a filmstrip, or completing an assignment. Most of the activities above involve voluntarism to a significant extent, yet most academic schoolwork is required and allows little room for choice. Most of the activities above rely on the individual's responsiveness in their shaping, yet most course syllabi are so heavily content-driven that there is no time to adapt material to student interests. ("That's an interesting question, Mary. Maybe we could look into that sometime. The next topic, class, is . . .")

The attribute of ownership, which encompasses so many characteristics of the activities in our list, is also largely absent from schoolwork. By and large, students do not choose what to study, nor how to study it, nor with whom. And as their own creative responses are ignored, they become increasingly alienated from the lesson and from the course of study. Because there is little sense of ownership in the inception of school activity, there is little pride of accomplishment in the outcome, as well as little sense of reward. There is also little opportunity for meaningful public display, little chance for a show of virtuosity. Also, most academic activity at school involves little physical activity, yet many of the situations in which we observe young people to be engaged involve some physical motion, often vigorous. In fact, most of what goes on in school runs counter to what our list would suggest about how best to engage the interest and curiosity of young people. Interestingly, those school activities that are most successful in engaging students tend to occur on the fringes of school life: clubs, sports, plays, the school newspaper, etc.

What steps should we then take? If our desire is solely to engage students, our job is simple. We will fill our school campuses with video-game parlors, cinemas, sports fields, and music studios. We will offer regular and frequent bus trips to the shopping malls and provide students with sufficient pocket money for cigarettes and hamburgers. We will stock the library mostly with the likes of *Rolling Stone*, *High Times*, fashion magazines, and sports magazines. We will enlarge the cafeteria and offer mostly junk food for consumption anywhere in the building all day long. We will fire all the teachers, except those with coaching experience, and bring in, to the extent that the budget will allow, visiting rock musicians, movie stars, models, beauticians, auto mechanics, and professional athletes. And we will let the kids do whatever they want. Most of the kids would love it (for a few weeks, anyway). Most would be said to be engaged.

But engagement is not all that we desire. We desire also that certain academic aims be met; that certain essential skills of inquiry and expression be mastered; that a certain core of knowledge, which we may call cultural literacy or common knowledge or whatever, be mastered; and that certain values be nurtured and others diminished. We do not seek mere engagement, we seek constructive engagement. We seek, as I have said, that elusive point of intersection between student interests and academic aims, that ideal lesson. Moreover, we should try to create an environment in which that kind of lesson and curriculum may thrive.

"What the fuck, man. What else are you gonna do?" Brian is trying to convince Donny, whom he has just awakened, that he may as well pay attention to Mr. Nehring, who is trying to start class. But Mr. Nehring is also listening to what everybody in the room, now seated in a circle of twelve, is saying to one another. And he is sort of getting the feeling by the looks of some of the quieter members of the class that the choice of words of some of the louder members of the class ought to be made an issue by Mr. Nehring. Mr. Nehring is wondering how to make it an issue without making it such a big one that everybody will get upset and lose what potential interest they may have in the lesson. Mr. Nehring decides to speak up.

"Listen, guys, there's a limit to the kind of language that is okay to use in this class."

"Oh, come on, Mr. Nehring. Be cool," says Rosemary.

"I have no problem with being cool, Rosemary. But I do have a problem with the regular use of offensive language when I can do something about it."

"What's offensive?" asks Rosemary. Everybody stops, waiting to see if Mr. Nehring will say it.

"Certain words . . . like *fuck*. Are you happy that I said *fuck*? I can say it all day long, but I don't, because it's offensive, at least to some people."

"So who's offended? Anybody here offended when I say *fuck*?" Rosemary looks around. Nobody answers. "There. See, Mr. Nehring?"

"I'm offended. Sometimes." I finally say.

"Oh," says Rosemary.

"But it isn't just the word, Rosemary. It's the way it gets used. It's mean. It says you don't respect someone or what he's doing."

"Okay, Mr. Nehring, you win. No more . . . you-know-what in class."

"Okay." I smile. "Here's the plan for today. I want you all to take ten minutes to skim the story you read yesterday and then complete the questions in Exercises A and B at the end. When everyone's done, I'll call on individuals to answer questions. Then we'll go right to the big question that I told you we were going to try to wrestle with today and that was: Was it right for the United States to drop the atom bomb on Hiroshima and Nagasaki? The only reason we're doing the exercises first is because I want to make sure everybody has a handle on the story before we move to the big question.

"Okay, everybody with me? Anybody *not* understand what we're going to do?" Silence. "Alexis, what are you supposed to do now?"

"Uh, I'm supposed to like read this." She points to the story. "And I'm supposed to do some questions or something."

"Right," I say. "Which questions, Rebecca?"

"Ahm, the ones at the end . . . A and B."

"That's right, Rebecca. Good. Esther, why am I having you do the questions?"

"Because you wanna see if we get the story."

"Right, good. You have ten minutes, everybody. Ready, go."

By this time of day a kid's mind is quick to wander from where I want it to be, so I continually need to monitor whether the words coming out of my mouth are registering in their brains. The group falls silent. Everything's registering. Something, at least, has registered. I observe their faces. Intent, engaged. I am happy.

I savor these moments when students are deeply, meaningfully, educationally engaged because they are less frequent than they ought to be. At no time is this fact more apparent than at the end of the school year, when the chaos that has swirled under the school's appearance of orderliness breaks through in an almost ritual manner.

Such as with the senior "prank" four years ago. The cafeteria had been in its usual state of uproar during A lunch on the last Wednesday of the year. There had been rumors afoot for several days that certain members of the senior class were plotting something. At the appointed moment, from several locations within the cafeteria, amid the noise and activity, a good two score of white laboratory mice were released onto the floor. As panic quickly hit table after table, a diversion was created, making it possible for certain other members of the senior class to usher through the emergency exit a certain additional creature that had been held off in the wings until just the right moment: a skunk, which was mightily and justifiably frightened at the sight of the cafeteria and commenced to race frantically about the floor, stopping only to rear up and leave its scent on certain unfortunate victims whose only offense was wishing to eat their lunch.

All of this was unknown to me as I ate my lunch in the faculty lounge at the other end of the building. Lunch ended. I walked up to Room 25. No kids in sight. Odd. I opened the door. Waited in the hallway. Still no kids. Slowly they started to arrive. The late bell rang and only half the class was present. I left the hall and walked to the room. There, a dozen or so ninth-graders looked up in silent anticipation like runners eyeing the starter, waiting for his trigger finger to jerk, release the hammer, and fire the gun.

"So what happened?" I ask. Like runners at the sound of the gun, my ninth-graders were off with a dozen versions of the big event in the cafeteria, all trying to shout louder than the other kids and get Mr. Nehring's attention. I knew this was going to happen and smiled as much at their response as at my satisfaction for having accurately predicted it.

"Wait!" I wave my hands. "Let's hear *one* story." I search the crowd for a reporter with credibility. "Erin, you tell me what happened. And don't anybody say anything until Erin is completely finished."

"Well," Erin begins, "everybody was eatin' their lunch like normal, and everything's just fine, see? All of a sudden there's all these white mice on the floor and all the girls are like screamin' and going 'Oooh' "—the group laughs at Erin's imitation of girls shrieking at mice—"but that was just a distraction because all of a sudden there's this skunk and somebody let it in from the emergency exit while all the mice were distracting everybody, see? And the skunk starts spraying, and Alison Weekes got sprayed. You should've seen her scream, 'Eeeeek.' " Erin is disappointed that the class doesn't respond as well to his second dramatic attempt. "So, anyway, then the principal comes in, and boy, was he mad, and he's yellin' for everybody to go out the emergency exits and so that's what we did, and then they wouldn't let us back in and that's why we're all late."

"And boy, am I hungry! They wouldn't even let us eat our lunch," says Karrey McConnell.

"Yeah," says the group.

What to do with a dozen hungry ninth-graders when the topic for the day is supposed to be final-exam review? My first strategy is to ignore their plight, figuring that it is more symbolic than real. A mistake.

"Okay, everybody. I'm sorry you're hungry but there's not a whole lot I can do about it. You all have a final exam in three days and you've got a lot to do to get ready for it." Lots of mumbling around the room. "So take out your index cards, get in your groups, and as you finish the cards, bring them up and I'll give you more." They had started making flash cards the day before.

"Oh, Mr. Nehring!" they chorus.

"Sorry," I say.

They comply reluctantly. Then, about five minutes into index cards, Karrey McConnell looks up from her seat and cries, "Oh, Mr. Nehring, I'm *so* hungry!" And I am a sucker for big round pleading eyes.

"Well, here, have a breath mint," I offer.

"Oh, thank you, Mr. Nehring." Karrey always talks like she's overacting her part in the school play.

"Hey, Mr. Nehring." This is Betsy Almindero, who approaches my desk with a conspiratorial whisper. "I have some food in my locker."

"Okay, just be discreet. And don't leave any wrappers on the floor. And share it." Betsy is out and back in a flash.

She starts passing out handfuls of nourishment (of an unknown nature) to her classmates, who receive them with heartfelt thank-yous. This is great, I reason. The kids will stop thinking food and start thinking index cards.

No such luck. Unknown to me, Betsy has passed out a bagful of fireballs, and within moments I am besieged by red-mouthed students who have quite forgotten their hunger under pain of fireballs, and who in an effort to convince Mr. Nehring that they really must go at once to the drinking fountain are sticking out their tongues and showing off their very red mouths as proof.

Bill Pierce is right. School is a three-ring circus. The end of the school year only makes plain this essential nature. And the metaphor is sadly apt. The school day is often little more than a parade of clownish acts that entertain more than they enlighten. Society recognizes this and to an extent condones it.

The scene is commencement three years ago at Amesley. The president of the Board of Education steps to the microphone. Already during the introductory remarks by various school and community figures there has been much catcalling, noisemaking, and general hoopla. The rabbi's invocation was interrupted by an anonymous cry from among the graduates, "Cut the crap, already!" Board President Alice Jakowics begins to address the group. All of a sudden balloons appear from under graduation gowns and commence bouncing above the heads of the audience. Several land on the stage. Jakowics smiles, laughs, picks up a balloon, tosses it back to the graduates. A playful volley ensues. Diplomas are handed out. The band plays "Pomp and Circumstance."

Since the incident with the white mice, George Handelman had been narrowing the field of suspects. Turns out several kids had been injured in the rush for the exits and there was talk of pressing charges against the conspirators. One parent called to say she heard her son was being told that his graduation would be delayed because he was suspect, and how she felt this was really going overboard because it was a harmless prank and she had even thought it pretty clever when her son and some of his friends had planned it out one afternoon at her kitchen table.

She served brownies, she said.

English Eleven Slow reads. Ten minutes is up. I ask rote questions. They offer rote answers. They say this is boring. I agree and tell them it's necessary. Then it's time for the big question that all the reading, skimming, rote questions, and rote answers have been leading up to.

"Do you think it was right for the United States to drop the atom bomb on Hiroshima?" I ask.

Silence.

More silence. Have you ever noticed the tension that mounts the longer a question goes unanswered? I have. And I've noticed it can be a very useful thing for a teacher because it focuses attention. In educationese, the space between the question and the answer is called *wait time*. People who do studies of such things tell us that typically teachers wait about a second tops before calling on someone to express an answer. If somebody asked you about the rightness of the bombing of Hiroshima, could you answer in one second? What kind of a question could you answer in a second? What is the chemical composition of water? What is eight times thirteen? What did you have for dinner last night? What time is it? What is your name? Could you answer any of those in a second? Could you answer the previous question in a second?

So why don't teachers wait longer? Either (a) the questions are very simple to answer, which means that teachers ought to be asking harder questions; or (b) teachers don't want to wait. Why not wait? Well, if their kids are anything like mine, they're probably afraid of what might happen during that wait time. Alex could fart, Billy could belch. Mike could call Jason a dirtbag. Kim could say, "This class is beat." All of which would not contribute positively to the objectives of the teacher's lesson. But, truth be told, if it's a good question—meaning the kids have been given enough information to make up an answer—everybody's too nervous to fart, belch, or call each other dirtbags. They're all thinking about the question.

"Well," Dawn Jenko begins, "I think it was the right thing to do."

"Okay," I say with enough of a pause to dignify her answer. Then, "Why do you think so?" I ask as nonthreateningly as possible.

"Well, the war was going on and on, and this was a way to stop it."

"I don't think it was right," says Rosemary. "I mean, think of all those people . . . with their flesh melting off them . . . yuk, that's *so* gross."

Todd Lopez jumps in. "Yeah, but think of all the *other* people that woulda died if they didn't drop the bomb. I mean, like in the story where they say the war woulda like dragged on another year. This way all those people didn't die."

"Yeah, 'n' 'is way i' was cheaper," says Jay.

Alexis Lesandre speaks up. "Yeah, but like how do they know it was gonna last another year? I mean, they coulda been wrong, you know. Maybe the Japanese were about to surrender."

"Fat chance," says Todd.

"How do *you* know?" asks Alexis.

" 'Cause it said in the story. You know, where the little kid dying in the hospital says his people thought the emperor was *God*. They weren't about to give up."

"I think you're all sick," says Rebecca Thornton. "I mean, what were we doin' fightin' the Japanese anyway? Why not jus' leave 'em alone and mind our own business? That's the problem—we're always stickin' our noses in everywhere where it don't belong."

"Oh, okay," says Donny. "So you don't mind like if the Japanese wanted to take over America like they woulda done if'n we hadn't stopped 'em?"

"Well, that's different."

"What's the difference?"

"Well, we can like protect ourselves, but we shouldn't like go fightin' wars in other countries, ya know?"

"Yeah, and then by the time they get to our country, they're too big to stop."

Esther Paige speaks up. "I don't think we should've dropped the bomb."

"Why is that, Esther?" I ask.

"Well, I think we like could've warned them, you know, like dropped the bomb in the ocean just to show 'em what could happen and then tell 'em to surrender. I mean, just think about that poor little boy. He's only sixteen and he was already dying. I mean, that's like our age."

"Tha's war," says Jay.

"Oh, yeah, right," says Alexis. "How would you like to die at age sixteen?"

Jay shrugs.

So the conversation goes, pretty much under its own steam. I enter only when it seems a thought has been played out as far as it can go and a new direction needs to be established, or if one person is dominating. This is good, I think. Real good. Here my kids are carrying on a meaningful dialogue of their own accord, letting each other express their thoughts, challenging each other's opinions, supporting their own opinions, referring to the text from which all this talk has sprung, and speaking honestly, not just giving answers that the teacher wants to hear. I begin to feel affirmed in my efforts today. Any day contains small successes and failures, but it's nice, I think to myself, when the day ends with a success.

Pretty soon I'll go home, and tonight, after Laurie, my wife, gets home from work, we'll stand in the kitchen making supper. We'll drink a beer and Laurie will say, "Tell me some funny stories from school today."

I'll say, "I taught and they learned"—a timeworn finesse that entered these end-of-the-day kitchen discussions years ago.

Laurie will say, "Great, I was hoping for something uplifting. Something that might make me forget all the frustrations of office life."

I'll hem and haw, trying to recollect. By six o'clock, the workday is a dissolving blur. Then I'll probably start with lunch—what everybody talked about at lunch. Jerry Rubicon's list of eighth-grade disasters will be first. Then I'll mention the fire drill—during lunch—and how all the answers to the biology test got traded in the hallway. I'll probably mention my faux pas in homeroom when I mistook my overdue notice for a student's. I'll mention Amos Morley's box and my early-morning trip to George's office. And, of course, Eddie Hastings ripping the clock off the wall in ISS. My day at the circus.

This all will make Laurie forget her office frustrations. Then she'll say, "So tell me what your kids learned."

I'll hesitate again as I always do with this question. Sometimes it takes me a few minutes to fully remember what I taught. Good thing Laurie doesn't mind wait time. Mohandas Gandhi will be the lead story since it happened first, and then the research paper and how Dale, Candy, and Frank just wanted to do the research paper the way they're used to, and Laurie will say, "So did you let them?" and I'll say no, and Laurie will say, "Good!" Finally I'll tell about English Eleven S and how Jay and Rosemary and all the rest carried on a meaningful discussion about a story they read and the important issues it raised. Laurie will say that's good, too. And I'll say, yeah, that *is* good.

English Eleven Slow is still talking Hiroshima and atomic bombs, as they have been for a good twenty-five minutes.

"So what do *you* think, Mr. Nehring?" Rosemary calls me out of my reverie.

"Huh?"

"Do you think it was the right thing to do to drop the bomb on Hiroshima?"

"Yeah, what do *you* think, Mr. Nehring?" Tammy says.

What I think is that this is a switch—my students asking me for my opinion. It's usually the other way around. Indeed, it seems that all those education courses stressed that I, the teacher, should never offer my opinion to my students, for it would bias their thinking. Always stand aloof, force your students to think independently, challenge their assumptions. Good stuff, I guess, but it's unrealistic. After all, if these matters we discuss are real and important, then I ought to have an opinion about them. Our discussion is not just a classroom exercise, it is—or is supposed to be— an extension of life. And I am not a purveyor of answers but a participant in the business of finding solutions, just like my students. Therefore if I stand aloof from the discussion, I will reinforce the illusion that it is just an exercise, something about which I *may* remain aloof. But it is not, and therefore neither should I stand aloof.

"What do I think?" I repeat.

"Yeah," says Todd. My students wait. They would be good teachers.

"Well, I'm afraid I cannot give a straightforward yes or no. On the one hand, how could you ever say it's right to do something which you know would result in the kind of pain and destruction described in the story? On the other hand, as Todd pointed out, not doing so might have resulted in more pain and destruction. I guess at a deeper level the question is whether the use of violence is ever justified. I mean, even if your reasons are good and your enemy is the worst, most evil kind of person imaginable, is it ever okay to inflict violence? I'm not saying the Japanese were evil—it's hard to imagine that little boy in the story had anything to do with Japanese imperialism—but that's sort of the underlying question. And I guess another underlying question is: In a war, who really is the enemy? Is it the soldiers bearing the guns? Is it the presidents and kings who give the orders? Is it the financiers and capitalists whose power dictates national policies? Is it the people, who carry out the policies of the rich and powerful without protesting?"

"You don't seem too sure of yourself there, Mr. Nehring," says Todd.

"I guess I'm not, Todd. Would you be sure of yourself if you had to make a decision like dropping the bomb on Hiroshima?"

"Well, ya got a point there. But still, somebody had to decide that."

"That's right," I say.

The bell rings. Nobody moves. Wait time.

"We'll see you all tomorrow," I finally say. The group heads to the door. I follow.

"So, Rosie," says Todd, "what would you do, anyway?"

Rosemary answers, "Well, I don't know. Like Mr. Nehring said, I don't know if it's ever right to use violence."

They head through the doorway. Brian jogs up to Todd and Rosemary and walks abreast of them.

Brian says, "Oh, that's bullshit. Sometimes you just gotta do what you gotta do."

Rosemary says, "Yeah, but like, you know, do you really gotta do it, is the question. Do you think it's right that some little kid gets blown away like that?"

Todd says something, assertively aiming a finger at the ground, but I can't make out what he says, as their voices get lost in the din of the hallway. Brian gestures urgently at Rosemary. Rosemary points a finger in the air and makes a reply. They turn the corner, out of view.

But the discussion, I like to believe, goes on. Part of a larger discussion that really began before Socrates and the Agora and the School of Athens. A discussion that encompasses all great human issues and is the very pulse of human culture. That our students keep this discussion going after they leave our classrooms is the measure by which our schools will be judged. It is, after all, why we gotta do this stuff.